CONTEMPORARY NEW ZEALAND POETS IN PERFORMANCE

CONTEMPORARY NEW ZEALAND POETS
IN PERFORMANCE

EDITED BY JACK ROSS & JAN KEMP

Jan Kemp

To the Centre for New Zealand Studies, London – warmest wishes to all your listeners & readers. on behalf of the poets, JK. July 2008 Florence

AUCKLAND UNIVERSITY PRESS

First published 2007

Auckland University Press
University of Auckland
Private Bag 92019
Auckland
New Zealand
www.auckland.ac.nz/aup

ISBN 978 1 86940 395 9

National Library of New Zealand Cataloguing-in-Publication Data
Contemporary New Zealand poets in performance / edited by
Jack Ross & Jan Kemp.
Includes bibliographical references.
ISBN: 978-1-86940-395-9
1. New Zealand poetry—20th century. I. Ross, Jack, 1962-
II. Kemp, Jan, 1949-
NZ821.208—dc 22

Publication is assisted by creative nz

Cover design: Christine Hansen
Cover image: Richard Killeen, *Red Insects Blue Triangles*, 1980, oil stencil on paper.

Printed by Kyodo Printing Company, Singapore

CONTENTS

Preface: Voiceprints   ix
Acknowledgements   xiii

PETER OLDS   Waking up in Phillip Street   1
                             Doctors Rock   2
                             Elephant   3
                             Biography / Selected Bibliography   5

BERNADETTE HALL   Party Tricks   7
                             The Lay Sister   8
                             Famine   9
                             Amica   10
                             Biography / Selected Bibliography   10

STEPHANIE DE MONTALK   Tree Marriage   12
                             Northern Spring   13
                             Biography / Selected Bibliography   15

ALAN BRUNTON   The Man on Crazies Hill   17
                             from Waves   20
                             Biography / Selected Bibliography   24

SAM HUNT   My Father Scything   26
                             Rainbows and a Promise of Snow   26
                             Hey, Minstrel   28
                             from Plateau songs   29
                             Bottle to Battle to Death   31
                             Biography / Selected Bibliography   32

BILL MANHIRE   The Old Man's Example   34
                             Domestic   34
                             On Originality   35
                             Visiting Mr Shackleton   36
                             Miscarriage   37
                             Valedictory   37

.

	A Song about the Moon	38
	Biography / Selected Bibliography	39
JAMES NORCLIFFE	at Franz Josef	42
	planchette	43
	the visit of the dalai lama	44
	Biography / Selected Bibliography	45
IAN WEDDE	Earthly: Sonnets for Carlos 31	46
	Earthly: Sonnets for Carlos 32	46
	Earthly: Sonnets for Carlos 35	47
	Barbary Coast	48
	Biography / Selected Bibliography	51
FIONA FARRELL	Anne Brown's Song	53
	Instructions for the Consumption of your Humanitarian Food Package	54
	Biography / Selected Bibliography	56
KERI HULME	*from* Fisher in an Autumn Tide	58
	Biography / Selected Bibliography	61
MURRAY EDMOND	Voyager	63
	Biography / Selected Bibliography	68
JAN KEMP	Against the softness of woman	69
	Jousting	70
	The sky's enormous jug	70
	Sailing boats	71
	'Love is a babe . . .'	72
	Biography / Selected Bibliography	72
CILLA MCQUEEN	Living Here	74
	Fuse	76
	Biography / Selected Bibliography	77
BOB ORR	The X	79
	A Country Shaped like a Butterfly's Wing	80

	Ballad of the Great South Rd	81
	Eternity	82
	Biography / Selected Bibliography	83
GEOFF COCHRANE	Spindrift Sunday	84
	1988	84
	Zigzags	85
	Atlantis	86
	Biography / Selected Bibliography	87
BILL SEWELL	Jahrhundertwende	88
	Riversdale	88
	Breaking the quiet	89
	Censorship	91
	Biography / Selected Bibliography	92
DAVID EGGLETON	Poem for the Unknown Tourist	94
	Teen Angel	95
	Biography / Selected Bibliography	96
GRAHAM LINDSAY	Playground	98
	Cloud silence	99
	Life in the Queen's English	100
	Chink	101
	Biography / Selected Bibliography	103
IAIN SHARP	Amnesty Day	104
	Two Minute Poem	105
	Biography / Selected Bibliography	107
JANET CHARMAN	'they say that in paradise'	108
	ready steady	109
	from wake up to yourself	110
	but she wanted one	111
	cuckoo in the nest	112
	injection	113
	Biography / Selected Bibliography	114

PAULA GREEN   greek salad   115
     oven baked salmon   115
     afternoon tea with Virginia Woolf   115
     Two Minutes Westward   116
     Biography / Selected Bibliography   118

VIVIENNE PLUMB   A Letter from my Daughter   119
     The Vegan Bar and Gaming Lounge   120
     The Tank   121
     Biography / Selected Bibliography   122

APIRANA TAYLOR   Sad Joke on a Marae   123
     Parihaka   124
     Hinemoa's daughter   125
     six million   126
     Biography / Selected Bibliography   127

ANNE FRENCH   The new museology   128
     Trout   130
     Acute   131
     Uncle Ron's last surprise   132
     Biography / Selected Bibliography   132

MICHELE LEGGOTT   cairo vessel   134
     Biography / Selected Bibliography   139

RICHARD VON STURMER   Dreams   141
     Biography / Selected Bibliography   145

ROMA POTIKI   Exploding Light   146
     For Paiki   148
     Riven   149
     Biography / Selected Bibliography   150

Track List   151
Variant Readings   154
Bibliography   162

PREFACE : VOICEPRINTS

Once it was decided that our spoken poetry anthology *Classic New Zealand Poets in Performance* might require not one but two sequels, we thought that it would be best if each of the three books had its own independent character, in keeping with the era it represents. This second volume, *Contemporary New Zealand Poets in Performance*, is our overview of the poetic generation which came to maturity in the 1960s and 1970s, that turbulent era of social, sexual, musical and artistic experimentation. These are the poets included in Arthur Baysting's pioneering 1973 anthology *The Young New Zealand Poets* (famously referred to as '18 men and Jan Kemp') and since surveyed in more depth by the anthology *Big Smoke* (2000), edited by Alan Brunton, Murray Edmond and Michele Leggott – not to mention Bernard Gadd's 'counter-anthology' *Real Fire: New Zealand Poetry of the 1960's and 1970's* (2001).

These poets were born during the post-Second World War baby boom, including no fewer than five born in 1946 – Bill Manhire, Ian Wedde and Sam Hunt among them. These three, along with Alan Brunton, Peter Olds, Bob Orr and Jan Kemp, are also the poets for whom we are fortunate enough to have two sets of recordings. Each of them read for the Waiata Archive in 1974 and six of them for the Aotearoa New Zealand Poetry Sound Archive in 2002–04.

We have been kindly assisted in filling the gaps in the otherwise comprehensive coverage afforded by these two archives (53 poets recorded in 1974, 171 poets in 2002–04) by the recordings made by both the New Zealand Electronic Poetry Centre (nzepc) and the Waitakere City Council's Going West Books and Writers festival, for which we make grateful thanks.

⸺∞⸺

In projects of this sort, the most difficult thing is deciding whom to leave out. One of the decisions we made early on was to adhere to chronological arrangement by dates of birth, which has (unfortunately) ruled out various poets born before 1944 who might otherwise have found a place in this book. Diana Bridge (b. 1942), Wystan Curnow (b. 1939), Dinah Hawken (b. 1943), Heather McPherson (b. 1942) and Mark Young (b. 1941) are just a few of the names whose absence we regret.

Our principal criteria for selecting poets and poems remain, however:

- literary merit (inevitably a subjective category, but also the most important one);
- a strong body of published work (including at least one full-length collection of poems); and
- a commitment to performance and the living voice as an integral part of the work.

This last is particularly important to the poets of this era. Among these various new areas of freedom, language in itself was something to be celebrated. As well as the written word produced with all sorts of varying typography, the *spoken* word was being shouted out loud. There were masses of poetry readings all over the country, sometimes with huge audiences, and large print runs of poetry collections. As in *Classic New Zealand Poets in Performance*, these recordings serve to remind us that we are not always a silent people.

Our *Contemporaries* collection begins then with Peter Olds waking up in a seedy boarding house and follows through visions of home and away in its 87 tracks. We have Bill Manhire at once minimalist, wicked and ambiguously domestic (his persona being told to 'get on the end of' a tea towel). Ian Wedde's lush voyage ends with a vision of Icarus, and Alan Brunton's with the repeated dramatic line 'a stranger to my home'. Bob Orr, on the other hand, 'floating in blue space like a chrysalis' seems so much at home here that he could never be a stranger. Language is indeed a poet's home; but home can also be an era, as in the case of Geoff Cochrane's 'Atlantis' – an island of nostalgia forever melting away.

Sam Hunt, one of the singing troubadours of sexual conquest, is here too, recalling another well-established New Zealand tradition: man, woman, dog (woman gone, dog dead, man alone). Hunt's feat, apart from writing movingly to parents and friends and declaiming in his raspy lyrical voice, was to 'pull the poetry books off the shelves and bring the poetry to the people for whom it was written'. Keri Hulme might be seen as his polar opposite. She appears rarely in public but, as her poem here shows, she is a warm reader whose narratives of human lives intertwined with nature are equally accessible to a listener.

'Why is our art so introverted?' asks Graham Lindsay in 'Cloud silence'. Alan Brunton's phrase, 'to have a vision you must leave home', provides a partial answer, or at least explains the freedom of vision that motivated Brunton, Murray Edmond or Ian Wedde to write world-ranging poems. Here or there? A fresh and witty take on 'here' is given by English-born Cilla McQueen's 'Living Here', where she explains how each New Zealander lives surrounded by a flock of sheep. A more sombre reflection is supplied by James Norcliffe's search for the words to name things on Franz Josef glacier whilst thinking of Pol Pot's massacres.

The later female voices collected here seem more relaxed as writers than their sisters of the late 1960s/early 1970s. Compare the urgent stridency of Jan Kemp's 'Against the softness of woman' (written in 1971 and recorded in 1974) with her recordings from 2002. Paula Green's 'Two Minutes Westward' love poem, read in that breathy voice, breaking into Italian at a high point, is measured and confident. Michele Leggott's breath-taking rhapsody 'cairo vessel' exemplifies a sexual and emotional satisfaction and ease with the other, which we can now (perhaps) take for granted.

Stephanie de Montalk, Bernadette Hall and Fiona Farrell write deeply exploratory poems from a variety of perspectives, about family, nature, history. But look out for the kick. New Zealand women are the descendants of those who were the first in the world to vote. Their language use is as innovative and interesting as that of the male poets and their stance just as courageous.

Bill Sewell combines a sense for humanity and history moving through time with a fine aesthetic sense, while Lindsay sees the world in a grain of sand while 'tuning into the song of snails'. With David Eggleton, Iain Sharp and Richard von Sturmer we start hearing series of Frank O'Hara-like lists, yet another reminder of the big world outside – from Eggleton's rap mock-tourist-guide ironic take on New Zealand, to the journo's hard day's night of Glaswegian Sharp, to the Zen-like meditative images of von Sturmer, which he reads like single gong clangs. Similarly, Janet Charman, Anne French and Vivienne Plumb are all witty women working from domestic and family relationships as well as from the outside world, with a surreal touch and an arch in their voices.

Finally, Api Taylor's wail for his unknown language and substitution of the bottle for his lost tribal affiliation, 'Sad Joke on a Marae', is a sombre reminder that the Maoritanga movement with all its contemporary successes has still far to go. Our collection therefore ends on the word 'dispersed' in Roma Potiki's 'Riven' where, in the next life, her persona is finally 'freed to stare into the light all about me'.

To facilitate the use of the collection, we've listed CD and track numbers beside the text of each poem. Fuller details can be found in the bibliography and track list at the end of the book. Short biographies and bibliographies for each poet appear following their poems.

In some cases the poets have dated their own work. We have printed these dates in italics. Otherwise, the dates in square brackets after each poem record the date of its first book publication. In cases where the poem has not yet been collected in a book, we have tried to give the date of its first appearance in a periodical or online.

Once again, we've tried to be true to the words of the poem as it was read, rather than as its author published it (at the time or subsequently). All such variations between printed text and recording have been included in an appendix of variant readings (as was our practice in *Classic Poets*, we have confined this collation to published books and have not thought it necessary to extend it to periodical publications).

Once in Rome, through the window of a bus rounding a corner in a narrow street, Jan saw an image fixed inside a concave stone alcove – an open-mouthed terracotta face in relief – *la bocca de verità* – the mouth of truth. For us it's like that – the poet's voice. Not that it can ever be the voice of Truth, but it's the voice of the poet's own mouth, their own truth. This is what we've hoped to capture in this collection of recordings. We hope we've managed to communicate something of our own fascination with these human and poetic voiceprints.

Jan Kemp and Jack Ross, November 2006

ACKNOWLEDGEMENTS

Contemporary New Zealand Poets in Performance would not have been possible without the foresight and hard work of Jan Kemp, Jonathan Lamb and Alan Smythe, who put together the Waiata Recordings Archive (1974), but also without Professor Emeritus Mac Jackson, who suggested the Waiata collection and records in the first place.

Even more indispensable, this time around, were the materials from the Aotearoa New Zealand Poetry Sound Archive (2004), compiled and edited by Jan Kemp and Jack Ross, with assistance from Edmund King (who wrote the first drafts of many of the biographies included here) and Mark King (who collated the many audio files from many different studios). These recordings were collected by national coordinator Jan Kemp in Auckland, Elizabeth Alley in Wellington, David Howard with Morrin Rout in Christchurch and Richard Reeve with Nick Ascroft in Dunedin.

None of this could have been accomplished without the invaluable aid of staff and technicians at the following studios: SCAPA, University of Auckland; Vincent Geddes and the BBC World Service, Paparoa; Breaker Bay Records, Wellington; Braeburn Studio, Wellington; Plains Radio FM, Christchurch; Faculty of Arts, University of Otago; Arc Café Studio, Dunedin.

A very special thank you should go to Rose Yukich and Murray Gray of Waitakere City Council's Going West Books & Writers festival, who generously shared with us the riches of their archive of recorded readings over the years. Similarly, we are most grateful to Michele Leggott and the nzepc for allowing us to use their recordings.

Thanks are also due to all those people who allowed us permission to reproduce material: Ruby Brunton, Michele Leggott and Martin Edmond for the Estate of Alan Brunton; Janet Charman; Geoff Cochrane; Stephanie de Montalk; Murray Edmond; David Eggleton; Fiona Farrell; Anne French; Paula Green; Bernadette Hall; Huia Publishers; Keri Hulme; Sam Hunt; Jan Kemp; Michele Leggott; Graham Lindsay; Bill Manhire; Cilla McQueen; James Norcliffe; Peter Olds; Bob Orr; Otago University Press; Vivienne Plumb; Roma Potiki; Amanda Powell for the Estate of Bill Sewell; Puriri Press; Iain Sharp; Apirana Taylor; Richard von Sturmer; Victoria University Press; and Ian Wedde.

Continued thanks to the team at AUP: Elizabeth Caffin, for her unswerving support of the project; to Anna Hodge, for her meticulous editing; to Christine O'Brien, for her tireless promotion of this and other poetic causes; to Katrina Duncan, our stylish book designer; and Annie Irving, efficiency incarnate. Finally, thanks must go to master-technician Wayne Laird of Atoll Records and to Richard Killeen for allowing us to use his image on the cover.

PETER OLDS (B. 1944)

Waking up in Phillip Street

[CD 1.1]

This two-layered cake full of puking TV sets
knife-cuts & blood on furniture & desk I've
inherited from former tenants, the door
(with my private number on) burgled, raped:
evidence of past busts, horrible deeds, murder
& wax on the carpet from candles of other solitary
confinements.

I wish the kid bashing the shit out of
the drum-kit in the house over the back fence
would give it away & take up surfing or girls –
or Buddhism! (What's wrong with getting out
of the house occasionally, anyway?)

The drug-bag arsehole in the room below next to the
toilet smells out the house with a foul concoction
of plants from the southern cemetery boiling on
the stove – up all night jerking with some rented
holocaust abortion.

Ghosts at night on the stairs (lit by street lights)
plead for the noise to stop; stand in fading lace
staring at the Edwardian Grecian wallpaper & little
snowflake boats sailing in formation on a bright
Mediterranean ocean – when confronted claim they are
looking for Sandy, Robin, the kitten – a cigarette.

The thick glass doors cannot separate the nerves
of the house from the spluttering oversized joint
in the communal kitchen; or the cat-strangling stories
of fantastic binges in past glory boarding houses:
a network of cooks, dental experts, psychiatrists
loan sharks, sexologists, chemists, bludgers, sneaks
competing for bench space –

'You *cunt!*' yells a fellow tenant handing out mail
at the top of the stairs to any person who cares
to risk coming out of their room – 'where did *that*
card come from!' – like the house's some sort of
country you can keep track of, & nobody in it has
any right to intimacy – either side of sleeping hours.

[2003]

[CD 1.2] **Doctors Rock**

When I was knee high
to a tadpole
and you were older – my brothers
and I
climbed the steep Oxford hill
to touch your cold cheek.

As I recall, you said nothing,
but pointed obscurely
out over the Canterbury Plains
and pine forests
that murmured of hunters,
fearful guns and rabbits.

My brother left his socks
up on top of your bald head,
and Mother sent him back
to beg your pardon . . .

A great wind blew up one year –
do you remember?
The hen house and cow shed blew over.
It must have been quite a sight
to behold from your rocky perch:
hens and cows scattering hysterical

through the broken flattened fences
into the cover of bush.
Did you see me down there on the flat
playing in the branches of a fallen tree?
It was winter, you know . . .

As I get older, I remember you less –
but I do imagine your moss-beard
and keen eye for detail –
the way you still nod
your silent Grandad grin.

[1976]

Elephant

[CD 1.3]

A circus comes to town
on the back of a train
of hot ash & red paint;
& soon the big paddock

is full of poles, greasy
pigs & generators;
shouting caged men
running up & down ropes

nimbly tugging at canvas flaps,
the smell of fresh grass
trampled ground, sweet smelly
dung mixed with hay steaming

out of a body looking
like something
someone would eat;
buckets of water

& a chain around a leg
attached to a thick steel peg
belted into the ground,
with hand clapping

& thunder clapping
& pink faces looking up
into a meshed sun
following a bale of hay

into a large mouth
hanging on the end
of a lump of thick rope . . .
And now

the head takes a bow;
after ten buckets of water &
two bales of hay (relying
on memory & improvisation),

& with a pointed stick
up its arse, the elephant
is down on one knee &
then the other;

there's a gasp! – will he roll
over in the sawdust &
crush the woman in the pink
tights

flat?
will he stand on one leg &
go round like a sycamore seed?
will he spray water over

his hairy back & into
the dark bank of faces
just for a laugh?
The pinhole eyes

PETER OLDS

look frantic
(almost mad) –
someone wants something fast
over there;

the body lumbers in the direction
of the pointed stick
mounts a small star-painted
box till all its feet

cover the skimpy top
& its arse pokes out
like a giant fig
& the skin wrinkles till it can't

wrinkle any more – like a
pile of ash in a harsh light,
or a long red train
on a hot night.

[2002]

Born in Christchurch in 1944, Peter Olds grew up in Dunedin and Auckland, where he attended Seddon Memorial Technical College. He left school at sixteen and worked in a warehouse before taking up window dressing in a large retail store in downtown Auckland. Wanting to grow his hair long, he left window dressing and became a cook. He began writing in the mid-1960s after being influenced by folk and pop music.

In 1966 he took a train journey to Dunedin and met James K. Baxter in a coffee bar. Baxter encouraged his writing. After a spell in the Cherry Farm mental hospital he joined Baxter's commune in Jerusalem, on the Whanganui River, and taught Baxter how to eel and cook goat. In the early 1970s, Olds joined up with Trevor Reeves, of Caveman Press, and through that association published several collections of poetry over the following decade. He was active in the poetry-reading circuit in the 1970s. In 1978 he was awarded the Robert Burns Fellowship.

In 2005 Peter Olds was the recipient of a grant from the Janet Frame Literary Trust. He lives in Dunedin.

POETRY:

Lady Moss Revived. Dunedin: Caveman Press, 1972.

The Snow & the Glass Window. Dunedin: Caveman Press, 1973.

Freeway. Dunedin: Caveman Press, 1974.

Doctors Rock. Dunedin: Caveman Press, 1976.

Beethoven's Guitar. Dunedin: Caveman Press, 1980.

After Looking for Broadway. Christchurch: One Eyed Press, 1985.

Music Therapy. Paekakariki: Earl of Seacliff Art Workshop, 2001.

'Oh, Baxter is Everywhere': Some Dunedin Poems. Dunedin: Square One Press, 2003.

It Was a Tuesday Morning: Selected Poems 1972—2001. Christchurch: Hazard Press, 2004.

Poetry Reading at Kaka Point. Wellington: Steele Roberts, 2006.

The Mad Elephant. Paekakariki: Earl of Seacliff Art Workshop, 2006.

BERNADETTE HALL (B. 1945)

Party Tricks [CD 1.4]

for Jules

it pays
to have a party
trick or two
tucked up
your sleeve
like Patrick's
pavlovas
or his blood
red T-shirt
with the white
blazon BETRAYAL
& you did brush
out your long
blonde hair
for that boy
(I know, I know
he was a real dick)
& people did stare
at the pair
of you &
an American said
in a big voice
outside Le Café
in Worcester
Boulevard
'My god, boy,
you look just like
Tom Cruise!'
which was true
& the police

bugged our house
you said
because he was
dealing but
nothing can go
too wrong
I say
for a girl
who can raise
one scathing
black eyebrow
higher than
the other
& talk
like Donald Duck

[1994]

[CD 1.5] **The Lay Sister**

The lay sister slides her hands
through holy water. Chops
onions, carrots, celery

in that order. Splits
blocks of wattle. Her hands
are fat on the axe handle.

'Good God,' says the Bishop,
slipping another smoke ring
round the crystalline throat

of the Portuguese sherry
decanter. 'That woman
would knock you down as good

as look at you!' The lay sister
is as rough as guts, speaks
Irish rather than English,

sleeps through the mission,
eats by herself in the kitchen.
Sometimes however

they do let her answer
the door and it's 'Excuse me,
Reverend Mother, there's

a piano in the parlour'
(that's the given code word
for a man) and she not able

to keep herself from laughing
then, imagining knocking
a fine old tune out of him.

[2001]

Famine

[CD 1.6]

My mother's great-great-grandfather strikes
my father's great-great-grandfather in the face
with his fist and my mother's great-grandfather
stabs my father's great-grandfather in the chest
with a pitchfork. Broken harvest.
Then my mother's favourite uncle lays about
my father's favourite uncle with a club, we
womenfolk screaming for blood as he pushes
his head down under the water. I have added
my stone to the stones of the others, casting
them down from the bridge. Then I washed
my hands, thank God, of the lot of them,

stole the family horse and on the proceeds,
took my message of peace way down to the Antipodes.

[2001]

[CD 1.7]   **Amica**

for Joanna Margaret Paul

The house is a reliquary
of insects, flowers & fingernails
& this is rare, Amica, that you assume
with your Etruscan air its essence;
lying on the hill arch of your arm;
on a sarcophagus. Someone is whistling
in the kitchen, laying down new territory
with aluminium brightness. All the windows
are open. Ivory tides wash out, wash in
& you sing the mysteries: that love
is a gift; that nothing is ever lost;
that death is the centre of a long life.

[1989]

Bernadette Hall was born in Alexandra, Central Otago, at the end of the Second World War. Her father was born into a Protestant family in Northern Ireland and her mother's Catholic ancestors had emigrated from Dublin and Waterford, so there are intriguing tensions in her heritage. As a child she shifted to Dunedin where she was educated by the Dominican Sisters. She gained an MA (Hons) in Latin from Otago University and taught Latin and classical studies at a number of high schools, most recently Christchurch Girls' High School.

She came late to writing, her first book appearing in 1989. Since then she has published five books of poetry. Her poems feature in most major recent anthologies. As well as poetry, Hall has written plays, essays, short stories and book reviews. In 2002 she co-edited with James Norcliffe an anthology of Canterbury poems, *Big Sky*, published by Shoal Bay Press.

In 1991 she was writer in residence at Canterbury University. In 1996, she held the Burns Fellowship at Otago University and in 1997 represented New Zealand at the International Writers Community in Iowa City, USA.

Hall was poetry editor for *Takahe* for ten years. In 2004 she received an Artists in Antarctica award and travelled to the ice with her friend and collaborator, the Dunedin visual artist Kathryn Madill. In 2006 she was writer in residence at Victoria University of Wellington.

Hall recently moved from Christchurch right into a classic Kiwi myth, a bach at a beach in North Canterbury.

POETRY:
Heartwood. Christchurch: Caxton Press, 1989.
Of Elephants Etc. Wellington: Untold Books, 1990.
The Persistent Levitator. Wellington: Victoria University Press, 1994.
Still Talking. Wellington: Victoria University Press, 1997.
Settler Dreaming. Wellington: Victoria University Press, 2001.
The Merino Princess: Selected Poems. Wellington: Victoria University Press, 2004.
The Ponies. Wellington: Victoria University Press, 2007.

EDITED:
[with James Norcliffe]. *Big Sky*. Christchurch: Shoal Bay Press, 2002.
Joanna Margaret Paul. *Like Love Poems*. Wellington: Victoria University Press, 2006.

STEPHANIE DE MONTALK (B. 1945)

[CD 1.8]   **Tree Marriage**

When the dandy of Bath died
his mistress put dust

covers over his tailor
and wigmaker and left

his Palladian mansion
to live in a tree

surrounded by heartwood,
broad leaves and, no longer

in need of clothing,
admiration in a natural setting.

She bought an embroidery frame
on which to record her impressions

of silence, shade and the beat
of rain in the branches,

themes of soil and sky,
observations only possible

some distance from the ground,
abstractions she could work up

into tapestries
at a later stage.

★

The tree's girth was her temple
its limbs her romantic imagination –

all olive brown in the evening
and at dawn as pale and grey as King Arthur.

⋆

She also recovered her sense of theatre
and original freshness,

learnt to be patient
with lichen and rough skin

and careful with candles
and winter fires

which she lit
in small tins.

[2002]

Northern Spring [CD 1.9]

A thousand steps
beneath cathedral

and clean sun,
beyond the brush

of hazel and pine,
the Bevin boys

born in Station Street
a mile from the tracks

above the shop of a baker
who made the best pies

ever tasted
wonder whether they should

mow their green heaths
now that the daffodils

are starting to fade,
now that the buttercup

fields of rape seed
are knee high.

★

One laments the loss
of his motorbike

and RAF uniform
during the war;

the other his brief career
as a shepherd,

his border collie –
some say the best dog

for the job –
and small knowledge

of animal behaviour,
although it goes

without saying
that a sheep can remember

STEPHANIE DE MONTALK

a fair life
and more than fifty human faces.

*

New leaves
over shale and soft water,

new winds
on the weather report.

*

Aspirin
to thin the blood.

Sotolol
to slow the heart.

[2002]

Stephanie de Montalk was born in 1945. She lives in Wellington and has four adult children. A registered nurse, she has also worked as a documentary film maker, video censor and warden of two university halls of residence. From 1996 to 2002 she was a member of the Film and Literature Board of Review.

She was educated at the Wellington Hospital School of Nursing and Victoria University, from which she graduated in 2000 with an MA (with Distinction) in creative writing.

She started writing in 1997. That year she was joint winner of the Novice Writers' Award in the BNZ Katherine Mansfield Memorial Awards. She was also joint winner of the Victoria University Prize for Original Composition in 1997.

In 2000 her first collection of poetry, *Animals Indoors*, was published by Victoria University Press. The following year it won the Jessie Mackay Award for Best First Book of Poetry at the Montana New Zealand Book Awards.

In 2001 her memoir/biography *Unquiet World: The Life of Count Geoffrey Potocki de Montalk* was published by Victoria University Press. It was published in Polish by Jagiellonian University Press, Cracow, in 2003.

In 2006 her first novel, *The Fountain of Tears*, was published by Victoria University Press.

POETRY:

Animals Indoors. Wellington: Victoria University Press, 2000.

The Scientific Evidence of Dr Wang. Wellington: Victoria University Press, 2002.

Cover Stories. Wellington: Victoria University Press, 2005.

PROSE:

Unquiet World: The Life of Count Geoffrey Potocki de Montalk. Wellington: Victoria University Press, 2001.

The Fountain of Tears. Wellington: Victoria University Press, 2006.

ALAN BRUNTON (1946–2002)

The Man on Crazies Hill [CD 1.10]

i

she drunk, man
      she drunk
no less than Polish spirit

used to see her come crawling
      up Hobson St
somebody was mean & bust
  a vein in her head
      she gets to her feet
in Freemans Bay
singing a sound the beginning
      was freedom
        & the end was
crying, crying

my son, he died in the shadow
of the moon
      rode away in the first
truck he could reach the door

      woman,
she drunk, man
      on her knees
in the coldbelly night
Polish spirit she carries
      in a plastic bag
& when it done,
      that bag just
gonna carry her away
  she talking to it, talking
to the horse in the dealer's yard

praying in Freemans Bay
      my son will come again

ii

what have you done, done
    said the girl
      (she rode like an
old grey mare) but it's not unkind
    the way she
      asks like that

Hey child, i have made you
    a natural woman
don't cry, i sleep
      between newspaper
leaves –
    i have seen you across
      the desert
& you are never coming back
    i know you cannot
steady go with me

i unhitched yr pocket
    & put some pennies in
      i have a ticket now
yet i might
      send you one –
    & whatever i have done
i never took you for yr better

    watch my ship as
it curls away from sight
    look twice & not turn
      back again,
no longer can i be rode
    with such excellent results
& without some damage
on such a onenight stand

iii

old woman plays the horses
   father on the harbour
he's painting his ship black
below the water line
cousin's in the cupboard
     & i'm sitting here stoned
i'm a stranger
       stranger
to my home
     but i play the harp
       after a style that
can say my southern name

i'm talking to cathode lady
   she's the one who is there
after the television station
     has closed down
& she points me
      faraway from here
& i will go, i
      won't be coming back
but the distance will be lonely

   i will send money so
old woman can play the horses
     put a needle
in my pack, & father harvest
   kelp with cousin micky finn

when i, dressed in turkish boots
   i'll send no letter
rather cross the marketplace
     without a name, be a
stranger,
     stranger to my home

[1973]

from **Waves**

so you want to know
Memm
lend undestructed ears,
I can do this ha ha only once . . .

In a single shack by candlelight
out back among
the muters of Brightwater,
a kaka in flight between the window
and the golden moon
the Earthly Guest
was born,
his mother dreaming
'beautiful as a wreck of paradise'
in her skirt of dust
beneath the open sky that night,
dreaming her little anomaly
on a mallow eating fire,
morning star and vesper star,
the tear of light,
dreaming I over I
that is geometry
and dreaming him
what always is
the Unremembered Dream
where One
in a black cloud
comes upon the unrepresented world
beginning as a 'grainy glow'.
His papa was a hurrying man,
hurrying from the swingle at the mill
in Shem's tent-city
on Wailing Creek
where it meets Burning Creek
where
Glossopteris grows

and he swinked for swinish gods.
The poebird flew above him
in the beeches as he ran –
Hurry hurry!
Ernest neither heaven learned nor chaos
from his father's lips

>　. . . the nuclear complex,
>　interested in that,
>　eh Memm

Rutherford picked up magnets
lying on the Urth and melaphyres,
and,
lying in a sack at night,
picked up transmissions from Siberia,
every March
when turnstones filled the sky;
he was the odd bod at school,
sometimes, in the middle of a match
he hunkered down
to draw universals in the sand,
like Archimedes, qed:
'if a quantity once moves it never rests'.
He was good,
he was keen,
E.R., Head Boy
valedictorian and dux
and set for bigger things,
that part of the planet was flat,
not wide enough for his Abode.
When he made his way to Canterbury
the dew was still
clinging to the grass.
They gave him the gownroom
in that godly city
to work at *solve-&-coagula*
with copper wires and sealing lacs

for he was
'Diligent in the use of his hands'

       you don't need the Band of Hope
       it stands to reason,
       Memm
       if you know the question
       the world's all continuity
       along parameters set centuries ago,
       you need no glazed
       optic tube
       Memm, to tell you that

As far as he could go at that time,
E.R. with air in his purse
at the edge of the expanding Empire
out, breaking up the clods
like Hesiod,
hoeing the haulms with a scuffle
in the black frost before sunrise,
stretched out in his dickey
in the dirt,
alone and elemental,
but as the sun influenced the sky
his brother came hippity-hop
in his iron boot
his shadow stuttering behind,
'Ernie, there's this letter.'
Standing, he tore the seal:
       'Greetings
       Rutherford,
       The Crystal Palace wishes to assist you
       in the ultimate attainment of your
       beehood
       please make an exhibition of yourself
       before the Queen
       &c., &c.'
In that ploughed field that day

prime matter opened,
E.R. chucked down his spade and damned
'That's the last spud I'll ever dig!'
from the tennis-court
farewelled his Ma
his fingers popping
and beggared down the quickened road
bound for Bassorah

      you could say
      Uranos was looking out
      Memm,
      looking for his boy

On the burning deck
To England O
far from the meridional stooks of ambrite
where Nestor's sails were furled
To England
via the service of the Ocean
To Englan
with his 'radi   os'
To Engla
on a ship with hoggets stacked below
To Engl
cursing P & O
To Eng
to live for six weeks at Humid Way
non fingo
To En
during a heat-wave in Sunny South Kensington
he slipped on a banana peel ha ha
rickety knees for the rest of his life!
To E.
R. came the gram from J.J.:
'Come to Cam and live with us,
campestral in the Fen.'
He always went the shortest distance,
walked to Cambridge in a week.

Rooming in Trinity
he could smell the neutrinos
on his nose,
just like that,
dropping from a Magellanic cloud . . . .

1994

Alan Brunton was born in Christchurch in 1946 and educated at Hamilton Boys' High School, the University of Auckland (where he took a BA) and Victoria University, Wellington, from which he graduated MA in English in 1968. He had begun to publish poetry while still a student and in 1969 founded the magazine *Freed*, funded by the Auckland University Students' Association. Five issues appeared between 1969 and 1972 (Brunton co-edited the first two). *Freed* combined poetry, essays and manifesto editorials with visuals, fonts and layout that reflected contemporary modes in art and graphic design.

In 1970, Brunton left New Zealand, travelling to Australia, India, Nepal, Afghanistan, Europe, Morocco and Britain, where his first collection, the chapbook *Messengers in Blackface*, was published in 1973. Returning to New Zealand the following year after more travel in South-East Asia, he and partner Sally Rodwell established the avant-garde theatre troupe Red Mole, for which Brunton would eventually write over forty scripts. In the mid-1970s, Brunton also co-edited the arts magazine *Spleen* for Red Mole Enterprises. Red Mole and its offshoot White Rabbit Puppet Theatre performed all over New Zealand between 1974 and 1978, and in 1979–87 were based variously in New York City, London, New Mexico and Amsterdam. Returning to New Zealand in 1988, Brunton based himself in Wellington, where he co-founded Bumper Books and worked as an editor, performer, director and arts community activist, while regularly contributing poetry and criticism to literary magazines. In 1998, he was writer in residence at the University of Canterbury. Brunton died in June 2002, while touring in Amsterdam with Red Mole.

POETRY:
Messengers in Blackface. London: Amphedesma Press, 1973.
Black & White Anthology. Christchurch: Hawk Press, 1976.
Oh, Ravachol. Greenhithe: Red Mole, 1978.
And, She Said. New York: Red Mole, 1984.
New Order. New York: Red Mole, 1986.
Chant of Paradise. Taos, NM: Red Mole, 1986.
Day for a Daughter. Illustrations by Sally Rodwell. Wellington: Untold Books, 1989.
Slow Passes, 1978–88. Introduction by Peter Simpson. Auckland: Auckland University
    Press, 1991.
Ephphatha. With Richard Killeen. Auckland: Workshop Press, 1994.
Romaunt of Glossa: A Saga. Wellington: Bumper Books, 1996.

33 Perfumes of Pleasure [CD]. Alan Brunton and the Free World Band, 1997.
Heaven's Cloudy Smile [video]. With Michele Leggott. Wellington: GG Films / Red Mole, 1998.
Moonshine. Wellington: Bumper Books, 1998.
Ecstasy. Wellington: Bumper Books, 2001.
Nietzsche / Zarathustra [CD]. Wellington: Red Mole / The Space, 2002.
Fq. Wellington: Bumper Books, 2002.

PLAYS:

Dreamings End. New York: Red Mole / Alexandra Fisher, 1984.
A Red Mole Sketchbook. Wellington: Victoria University Press, 1989.
Goin' to Djibouti: A Playscript. Wellington: Bumper Books, 1996.
City of Night [video]. Wellington: Red Mole, 2000.
Comrade Savage. Wellington: Bumper Books, 2000.
Grooves of Glory: Three Performance Texts. Wellington: Bumper Books, 2004.

PROSE:

Years Ago Today: Language & Performance, 1969. Wellington: Bumper Books, 1997.

EDITED:

The Word is Freed, nos 1–2 (1969–70).
[with Martin Edmond, Russell Haley and Ian Wedde]. *Spleen: A Magazine of the Arts*, nos 1–8 (1974–76).
Landfall 180: 'Hamilton Hometown' (December 1991).
Writing Island Bay. Wellington: Bumper Books, 1997.
[with Murray Edmond and Michele Leggott]. *Big Smoke: New Zealand Poems 1960–1975*. Auckland: Auckland University Press, 2000.
Sally Rodwell. *Gonne Strange Charity*. Wellington: Bumper Books, 2000.
The Brian Bell Reader. Wellington: Bumper Books, 2001.

SAM HUNT (B. 1946)

[CD 1.12] **My Father Scything**

My father was sixty when I was born,
twice my mother's age. But he's never been
around very much, neither at the mast
round the world; nor when I wanted him most.
He was somewhere else, like in his upstairs
Dickens-like law office counting the stars;
or sometimes out with his scythe on Sunday
working the path through lupin towards the sea.

And the photograph album I bought myself
on leaving home, lies open on the shelf
at the one photograph I have of him,
my father scything. In the same album
beside him, one of my mother.
I stuck them there on the page together.

[1972]

[CD 1.13] **Rainbows and a Promise of Snow**

for Alistair Campbell

I

Winter means one side or other of
the shortest day. Our birthdays both
are on that good side, friend, of
solstice. Winter is a warm hearth;

rainbows and a promise of snow.
Days go so fast, so slow.

It matters not. A good mate dies,
another goes abroad or mad.
It matters neither way. What does,
what always will, is that we load

the fire high with logs. She's a
winter this! bull-seals barking in the bay.
If she don't snow soon, I tell you
friend, she's never going to.

2

Sixteen, just left school
I dumped my books and hiked
four hundred miles south;
hitched-up where I liked:

barbaric coast, barbaric winds
madder than I knew could blow:
what better making of friends,
a promise of snow.

I go down to the river, friend,
walk along with the flow;
far as third bend,
far as I go:

remembering time goes
so fast, so slow:
solstice and birthdays,
a promise of snow.

A mad wind has risen,
the bull-seals bark at the moon:
I have a knee-high son;
you, a grandchild soon.

My chance to wish you cheers,
we've many good miles to go.
Here's rainbows (whisky tears),
a promise of snow.

[1980]

[CD 1.14] **Hey, Minstrel**

I know you're there.
I can hear you listening.

      Parked, say,
between a highway & river —
the roadbuilders left space
for dogs, & people like us.
The odd driver toots, spots
a man without a dog.
That's okay, you had to
die when you did.
We chose the day.
The day chose us.
It wasn't until after we buried you
there was any fuss.
Then it was Christmas.
I called up an old mate &
cut back on the piss.

I know you're there.
You came by last night
just as I was talking to
a woman with the moon in her hair.

Nothing unusual in that. The moon's
been hanging around
an awful lot lately.

But you were there for sure.
She kept asking if I was alright
& kept repeating her name
as if I didn't know her.

Strange, the times since you died.
But while there's space
for dogs & people, a place
a man can park his car
between a highway, say,
& a river;

        or, more simply,
touch the moon, then that's okay too.

[1995]

from Plateau songs

[CD 1.15]

for Tom, turning 11

I

I climbed the mountain to learn
I had no need to be there,
so took a room further down.
I could not have gone further.

I spend the most, most days now
inside of a hotel room –
a distant dad, a dizzy man,
on the edge of a mountain.

2

The lady at the pool table
has on a see-through dress.
Which is, I guess,
worth mentioning.

I mean, if she didn't
and I couldn't (see through it)
I wouldn't have thought
to mention it worth it.

3

A man asked me
last night in the house bar
just how it was
I could remember the poems.

I told him I could not forget them,
they're flesh and blood.
And your best poem? he asked me.
I told him Tom.

4

Your mother loved this plateau
country, Ruapehu.
Our best times were here
of three years together.

We never got to climb
or tramp or ski or do
what people do on mountains.
But she comes with the view.

[1989]

Bottle to Battle to Death

[CD 1.16]

for Kristin

Bottle to Battle to Death,
places where we lived from
meeting up one crazy night to
splitting up – a child in tow –
one nightmare of an afternoon.

Bottle Creek was our first home,
a boathouse perched on stilts.
The heron thought us one of them.
We paced the mudflats; full tide, swam:
no place (they said) to bring a baby up in.

To Battle Hill where once, one
hundred years before you or I were born,
a poet of a chief held back the Poms.
He let the land fight for him.
Our child was born here. Tom.

Those days, some days, were good,
the nappies flapping at the clouds,
the clouds crash-landing on the hills.
And white as mushrooms on the slopes,
the sheep; at lambing-time, the hawk.

We gave our child Kahu for
a second name, in honour of that hawk.
Our silences invaded us –
the dark hills, sky, the hovering.
It was, for us, an end of talk.

The move then down the valley,
back beside the estuary, the ancient
homestead, Death (and not De'Ath).
We didn't stand a chance.
We would stalk each other, minute by minute.

I would watch the shy pukeko. They
would run out on the road, crazy as
the clouds that charged the hills.
The cars would always win the game.
Pukeko dead, a dull blue flame.

And then, of course, there was you.
And to say I hated you was true.
And I loved you was true.
I thought though, if we lie down
low, we may come through.

Instead, minute by minute, we stalked
each other out. Sometimes we walked
the hills together, Tom in the back-pack,
the dog forever chasing sticks.
And then an afternoon, quite casually, I talked

of 'going our own ways'. I can't
remember now what brought me to it.
Maybe you said, we can't go on this way.
Or, maybe best we call it all a day.
I don't know now. But you went away.

[1982]

Sam Hunt was born at Castor Bay, on Auckland's North Shore, in 1946. He began writing
poems at age sixteen, influenced, he says, both by a family passion for reading and
reciting poetry and the musical and speech rhythms of early 1960s American singer-
songwriters.

In 1963, Hunt left St Peter's College, Auckland, and travelled to Wellington, where
among other people he befriended the poet Alistair Campbell (whose poetry he had
long admired). For the next four years, he oscillated between the two cities, working as
a panel-beater and truck driver and attending Wellington Teacher's College. He eventu-
ally graduated with a teaching diploma and taught briefly at a number of schools. By the
end of the 1960s he found himself living and working as a full-time poet. He became well
known for his performances in pubs, high schools, theatres, prisons and at festivals.

Hunt has always walked an individual path in the New Zealand poetic scene. He
categorises some of his works as 'road songs' rather than poems and, as well as more

conventional influences, for example the syllabic line of Thom Gunn, Hunt has continued to admire the work of songwriters like Bob Dylan and Patti Smith. His commitment to poetry performance and bringing it to the public remain the core of his work.

By the late 1980s, Hunt had become a familiar figure on television, as a presenter of documentaries and for his appearance in commercials. But he continued his long-time tradition of touring and performing, including a poetry road trip with Gary McCormick in the mid-1990s from which came the book *Roaring Forties*. A volume of new poems, *Down the Backbone*, appeared in 1995. Sam Hunt is currently working on a book of new and selected poems, *Doubtless*, to be published with Craig Potton, as well as a project called '100 poems of hate and an exit song'.

POETRY:

A Song About Her. Paremata: Bottle Press, 1970.
When Mornin' Comes (A Flat Fat Blues). Paremata: Bottle Press, 1970.
Bracken Country. Wellington: Glenbervie Press, 1971.
Letter to Jerusalem. Paremata: Bottle Press, n.d. [1971].
From Bottle Creek. Wellington: Alister Taylor, 1972.
South Into Winter: Poems and Roadsongs. Wellington: Alister Taylor, 1973.
Roadsong Paekakariki. Paremata: Triple P Press, 1973.
Time to Ride. Waiura: Alister Taylor, 1975.
Drunkards Garden. Wellington: Hampson Hunt, 1977.
[with others]. *Poems for the Eighties: New Poems*. Wellington: Wai-Te-Ata Press, 1979.
Collected Poems 1963–1980. Harmondsworth: Penguin, 1980.
Running Scared. Christchurch: Whitcoulls, 1982.
Approaches to Paremata. Auckland: Penguin, 1985.
Selected Poems. Ed. Michael Richards. Auckland: Penguin, 1987.
Making Tracks: A Selected 50 Poems. Christchurch: Hazard Press, 1991.
Down the Backbone. Auckland: Hodder Moa Beckett, 1995.
Roaring Forties. With Gary McCormick; photographer John McDermott. Auckland: Hodder Moa Beckett, 1995.

BIOGRAPHY:

Hogg, Colin. *Angel Gear: On the Road with Sam Hunt*. Auckland: Heinemann Reed, 1989.

BILL MANHIRE (B. 1946)

[CD 1.17] **The Old Man's Example**

These drifting leaves, for instance
That tap my shoulder
Come along with us, they say
There are one or two questions
We should like to ask you

[1972]

[CD 1.18] **Domestic**

She threw him the tea-towel.
Get yourself on the end of that.
What a strange woman!
Her novel had flowers in it,
a horse called Thunder,
but it never really sold.
Maybe not enough reviews,
maybe the wrong reviewers . . .
Strange woman, out in the kitchen,
chopping onions and dropping
bits down her butterfly front
as she wept and wept
and sustained it – thoroughly
losing the plot. So that was the end
. . . of what? . . . of *that*, if not
of the next little spell.
She came back through
and threw him the tea-towel.

[1999]

On Originality

Poets, I want to follow them all,
out of the forest into the city
or out of the city into the forest.

The first one I throttle.
I remove his dagger
and tape it to my ankle in a shop doorway.
Then I step into the street
picking my nails.

I have a drink with a man
who loves young women.
Each line is a fresh corpse.

There is a girl with whom we make friends.
As he bends over her body
to remove the clothing
I slip the blade between his ribs.

Humming a melody, I take his gun.
I knot his scarf carelessly at my neck, and

I trail the next one into the country.
On the bank of a river I drill
a clean hole in his forehead.

Moved by poetry
I put his wallet in a plain envelope
and mail it to the widow.

I pocket his gun.
This is progress.
For instance, it is nearly dawn.

Now I slide a gun into the gun
and go out looking.

BILL MANHIRE   35

It is a difficult world.
Each word is another bruise.

This is my nest of weapons.
This is my lyrical foliage.

[1977]

[CD 1.20] **Visiting Mr Shackleton**

for Chris Cochran

Cool! Wow! Beautiful! Awesome!
Like going back in time.
Amazing! Historic! Finally
I am truly blessed.

Wow! History! Fantastic!
Wonderfully kept.
Shackleton's the man!
Like going back in time.

Wow! Cool! Historic! Yo!
Awesome! Privileged. Unreal!
And Thank you, God. And Happy
Birthday, Dad. And Thailand.

[1998]

Miscarriage

[CD 1.21]

In the year most of the girls
started wearing bright colours,
my youngest daughter wore gray.
She sat up late, reading the paper,
nursing her terrible temper.

A lot of it slips
my mind now, but one night
her beauty slowly dawned on me;
then dawn came too
and her place was empty.

Where had she gone?
Was she lost in the headlines?
I think she must have slipped out
while I was reading something
over her shoulder.

[1991]

Valedictory

[CD 1.22]

Thank you for listening so patiently
to the poems that once made me famous.
I expect I rather run on. Now, let me turn
to and fro through the pages. Ah . . .

well, yes. And thank you for staying to hear
the one which might make me rich.
In a moment I will read it
and then after that we will be finished,

though poems, as I think you may know,
can go on and on lasting the distance, and sometimes
the reader will take them to heart, and thus
one's words grow a mite more accomplished,

clearer, yet . . . ah . . . far more mysterious,
like some last shot at happiness;
so that when, after the last somewhat desperate kiss,
you look up from the page,

well, the main thing surely you see is –
ah, here we are –
not the executioner's face
but his arms covered in bruises.

[1999]

[CD 1.23]   ## A Song about the Moon

The moon lives by damaging the ocean
The moon lives in its nest of feathers
The moon lives in its nest of clamps
The moon lives by aching for marriage
The moon is dead, it has nothing to live for

The bodies are dangerous, you should not touch them
The bodies resemble our own, they belong together
The bodies are weapons, someone will die of them
The bodies will not lack for wings, someone will find them
The bodies are maimed but you will not remember

Do you still suffer terribly?
Do you always speak French?
Do you stare at the moon for you cannot forget it?
Do you long to be emptied of nothing but feathers?
Do you want to go on like this almost forever?

You must abandon everything after all
You must abandon nothing at least not yet
You must abandon hilarity
You must abandon your flags
You must abandon your pain, it is someone else's

You must abandon poetry for you cannot forget it
You must abandon poetry, it never existed
You must abandon poetry, it has always been fatal
It is like the moon, it is like your body
It is like the ocean, it is like your face

[1982]

Bill Manhire is a Wellington poet, short-story writer, editor, anthologist and academic. Born in Invercargill in 1946, he grew up in small towns in Southland and Otago before moving to Dunedin. He attended Otago Boys' High School and the University of Otago, where he took a BA in English. After graduating, Manhire enrolled in the Department of Scandinavian Studies at University College, London, where he studied Old Icelandic. In 1973, after receiving his M.Phil., he returned to New Zealand to take up a lectureship in the English department at Victoria University, Wellington.

While a student at Otago, Manhire published his first poems in the *Otago University Review* and formed links with the Dunedin art and literary scenes. A friendship with the painter Ralph Hotere led to their collaborating on *Malady* (1970), Manhire's first book, and the formation of the Amphedesma Press, which published a number of small volumes by New Zealand poets in the early 1970s. (Manhire ran the press – in partnership with Kevin Cunningham – while living in London as a student.) He has since produced many further volumes of poetry, a 'choose your own adventure' novel, *The Brain of Katherine Mansfield* (1988), and a collection of essays and interviews, *Doubtful Sounds* (2000). He has also published numerous reviews and articles and edited a number of anthologies. In 1983, he took over the original composition course at Victoria; it has since expanded into a high-profile graduate programme offering an MA in creative writing. Since 2001, this has been run under the auspices of the International Institute of Modern Letters, of which Manhire is co-director. He has won the New Zealand Book Award four times and in 1997 was named New Zealand's inaugural Te Mata Estate poet laureate. In 2004, he was awarded the Katherine Mansfield Fellowship to Menton. He won the Montana New Zealand Book Award for Poetry in 2006 for *Lifted*.

POETRY:

Malady. Dunedin: Amphedesma Press, 1970.

The Elaboration: Poems. Drawings by Ralph Hotere. Wellington: Square and Circle, 1972.

How to Take Your Clothes Off at the Picnic. Wellington: Wai-te-ata Press, 1977.

Dawn/Water. Wellington: Hawk Press, 1979.

Riddles for Voice and Piano. By Gillian Whitehead. London: Photographic Service (Music Reproductions), n.d.

Declining the Naked Horse. Music by Mark Langford. Dunedin: University of Otago, Department of Music, 1981.

Good Looks. Auckland: Auckland University Press, 1982.

Zoetropes: Poems, 1972–82. Wellington: Port Nicholson Press, 1984.

The Old Man's Example. Wellington: Wrist & Anchor Press, 1990.

Milky Way Bar. Wellington: Victoria University Press, 1987.

My Sunshine. Wellington: Victoria University Press, 1996.

Sheet Music: Poems 1967–1982. Wellington: Victoria University Press, 1996.

[with Nigel Brown and Chris Orsman]. *Homelight: An Antarctic Miscellany*. Karori: Pemmican Press, 1998.

What to Call Your Child. Auckland: Godwit, 1999.

Collected Poems. Wellington: Victoria University Press, 2001.

Pine. By Ralph Hotere. Dunedin: Otakou Press, 2005.

Lifted. Wellington: Victoria University Press, 2005.

PROSE:

Maurice Gee. Auckland: Oxford University Press, 1986.

The Brain of Katherine Mansfield. Auckland: Auckland University Press, 1988.

The New Land: A Picture Book. Auckland: Heinemann Reed, 1990.

South Pacific. Manchester: Carcanet, 1994.

Songs of My Life. Auckland: Godwit, 1996.

Doubtful Sounds: Essays and Interviews. Wellington: Victoria University Press, 2000.

Under the Influence. Series editor Lloyd Jones. Wellington: Four Winds Press, 2003.

EDITED:

New Zealand Listener Short Stories. 2 vols. Wellington: Methuen, 1977.

[with Rachel Bush and Carol Markwell]. *Province: New Nelson Writing*. Nelson: Nelson Provincial Arts Council, 1987.

Six by Six: Stories by New Zealand's Best Writers. Wellington: Victoria University Press, 1989.

Soho Square. Four. Wellington: Bridget Williams Books, 1991.

[with Marion McLeod]. *Some Other Country: New Zealand's Best Short Stories*. Wellington: Unwin Paperbacks: Port Nicholson Press, 1984. New edition, 1992. 3rd edition, 1997.

100 New Zealand Poems. Auckland: Godwit, 1993.

Denis Glover. *Selected Poems*. Wellington: Victoria University Press, 1995.

1396, A Literary Calendar: 13 Works, Hand-set & Hand-printed. By 13 participants in Bill Manhire's 1996 Original Composition Class at Victoria University of Wellington. Wellington: Wai-te ata Press, 1996.

Mutes and Earthquakes: Bill Manhire's Creative Writing Course at Victoria. Wellington: Victoria University Press, 1997.

[with Karen Anderson]. *Spectacular Babies: New Writing*. Auckland: Flamingo, 2001.
The Wide White Page: Writers Imagine Antarctica. Wellington: Victoria University Press, 2004.
121 New Zealand Poems. Auckland: Godwit, 2005.
[with Paul Callaghan]. *Are Angels OK? The Parallel Universes of New Zealand Writers and Scientists*. Wellington: Victoria University Press, 2006.

JAMES NORCLIFFE (B. 1946)

[CD 1.24] **at Franz Josef**

struggling to remember
marble-leaf *carpodetus*
the white veins clear
against the upraised green

we hear Pol Pot has died again
but the reception is poor
the TV has cataracts double
vision and snow blindness

the heart of the glacier
is as hard cold and blue
as a carefully carried memory
ruthless and perfect

we step awkwardly
from boulder to boulder
talking of the killing fields
the crimes of a man

until we are as close
as the yellow guard rope
and heaving river will permit
and we stand there listening
for falling ice
                          trying
to remember the names
given to things
                      emperors
justice
            serrated leaves

[2003]

planchette

[CD 1.25]

at night the rats
are bigger than rats

they race back and forth
like typewriters
across the lath and plaster

like good little rats
they have taken their poison
and now they grow large with thirst

where are their pretty girlfriends
or love, the magician?

can not one of these
offer them solace or slake?

oh qwerty they clatter
oh qwerty qwerty

as the night grows hard round them
desperate in their scrabble

and the stars
set like teeth

[2005]

the visit of the dalai lama

for Bob

I've no idea whether
my uncle is a spiritual man

I only know that life
has battered him
as a fish is battered

and fried him
as a fish is fried

and rubbed salt
into all his wounds

but that when I say
how's the world

not bad he'll say not bad
and could be worse

just said with his mouth
looking elsewhere

papering himself
around with a warmth

that could steam windows

[1995]

James Norcliffe was born on 3 March 1946 in Greymouth. He has worked as an English teacher in Christchurch, China and Brunei, and now lives in Christchurch, where he teaches at Lincoln University.

His second collection of poems, *Letters to Dr Dee* (1993), was shortlisted for the New Zealand Book Awards in 1994 and his third novel for children, *The Emerald Encyclopaedia* (1994), was an honour award recipient at the 1995 AIM Children's Book Awards.

He has been an editor of *Takahe* (in various capacities) for many years and remains a member of the *Takahe* collective. He is currently the poetry editor of the Christchurch *Press* and president of the New Zealand Poetry Society.

He was the Robert Burns Fellow at Otago University in 2000 and writer in residence at the Hobart Writer's Cottage in Tasmania in July 2005. In 2006 he was a fellow of the International Writing Programme at the University of Iowa and a fellow at the Kimmel Harding Nelson Center for the Arts in Nebraska.

His sixth book of poems, *Villon in Millerton*, was published by Auckland University Press in June 2007.

POETRY:

The Sportsman and Other Poems. Auckland: Hard Echo Press, 1986.
Letters to Dr Dee. Christchurch: Hazard Press, 1993.
A Kind of Kingdom. Wellington: Victoria University Press, 1998.
Rat Tickling. Christchurch: Sudden Valley Press, 2003.
along Blueskin Road. Christchurch: Canterbury University Press, 2005.
Villon in Millerton. Auckland: Auckland University Press, 2007.

PROSE:

Under the Rotunda. Christchurch: Hazard Press, 1992.
Penguin Bay. Christchurch: Hazard Press, 1993.
The Chinese Interpreter. Christchurch: Hazard Press, 1994.
The Emerald Encyclopedia. Christchurch: Hazard Press, 1994.
The Carousel Experiment. Christchurch: Hazard Press, 1995.
The Past and Other Countries. Aotearoa New Zealand: New Zealand Chinese Writers' Association, 2000.
The Assassin of Gleam. Christchurch: Hazard Press, 2006.

EDITED:

[with David Howard]. *Left Hand Up a Bit*. Christchurch: Citron Press, 1990.
[with Glyn Strange, Colin Amodeo and Bill Nagelkerke]. *And Me for All of Those*. Christchurch: Clerestory Press, 2000.
[with David Howard]. *Passport Stamps*. Christchurch: Firebrand, 2001.
[with Bernadette Hall]. *Big Sky*. Christchurch: Shoal Bay Press, 2002.
[with Alan Bunn]. *Redraft* 2–4. Christchurch: Clerestory Press, 2002–2004.
[with Alan Bunn]. *Cupid on a Friday Night: Redraft* 5. Christchurch: Clerestory Press, 2005.
[with Alan Bunn]. *Tennis with Raw Eggs: Redraft* 6. Christchurch: Clerestory Press, 2006.

IAN WEDDE (B. 1946)

[CD 1.27] *from* **Earthly: Sonnets for Carlos**

31

Diesel trucks past the Scrovegni chapel
Catherine Deneuve farting onion fritters
The world's greedy anarchy, I love it!
Hearts that break, garlic fervent in hot oil
Jittery exultation of the soul
Minds that are tough & have good appetites
Everything in love with its opposite
I love it! O how I love it! (It's all
I've got

              plus Carlos: a wide dreaming eye
above her breast,
                 a hand tangling her hair,
breath filling the room as blood does the heart.

We must amend our lives murmured Rilke
gagging on his legacy of air.
Hang on to yours Carlos it's all you've got.

[1975]

[CD 1.28] **32** *dawn friday 17 august 1973 / American bombing halt in Cambodia*

The sky bellies
           in the east
               mouths of hills
spill thin milk, the Pleiades depart leading
their bull by the snout . . .

                    great Taurus drooling
for your Pasiphae
                    winched up on the sill
of Daedalus' weird machine, bollock-full
& red-eyed you gored & bellowed plunging
yourself asleep. Ah she was a strange thing

so foreign & delicate:
                    maddening you . . .
& that crazy egghead strapping you in . . .

Later you woke & saw monstrous children,
the cities crashing down. You were meant for
a gift, Bull, but you were hoarded & then
your huge   poison shot out into the world . . .

These are old tales Carlos
                    & there are more

[1975]

35 *in memoriam Pablo Neruda* [CD I.29]

   Pensando, enterrando lámparas en la profunda soledad

'Thinking, burying lamps in deep solitude'

where you are now señor
                    where no flag snaps
at the icy firmament
                    where no sap
of illumination shoots from the crude
masonry of the earth   ah Neruda

now you have become a lamp in that deep
sepulchre where the unending sleep
of generation dreams its beautiful
impure products

your poems here among them
whispering their own enigmas through the
spaces that were *your* ears   ah Neruda

you have no further use for your poems
but we need them we need them: let them be

green lamps that break

                                into our solitude

[1975]

[CD 1.30]   **Barbary Coast**

When the people emerge from the water
who can tell if it's brine or tears
that streams from them, purple sea
or the bruises of their long immersion?

They seem to weep for the dreams they had
which now the light slices into buildings
of blinding concrete along the Corniche.
Is it music or news the dark windows utter?

Day-long dazzle of the shallows
and at night the moon trails her tipsy sleeves
past the windows of raffish diners.
The hectic brake-lights of lovers

jam the streets. My place or your place.
They lose the way again and again.
At dawn the birds leave the trees in clouds,
they petition the city for its crumbs.

The diners are cheap and the food is bad
but you'd sail a long way to find anything
as convenient. Pretty soon, sailor boy,
you'll lose your bearings on language.

Language with no tongue
to lash it to the teller.
Stern-slither of dogfish guttings.
Sinbad's sail swaying in the desert.

Only those given words can say what they want.
Out there the velvet lady runs her tongue
over them. And she is queen of the night –
her shadow flutters in the alleys.

And young sailors, speechless, lean
on the taffrail. They gaze at the queen's amber
but see simple lamps their girls hang in sash windows.
Thud of drums. Beach-fires. Salt wind in the ratlines.

Takes more than one nice green kawakawa
leaf, chewed, to freshen the mouth
that's kissed the wooden lips of the figurehead
above history's cut-water

in the barbarous isles'
virgin harbours. That hulk shunned by rats
bursts into flames.
And now the smoky lattice of spars

casts upon the beach
the shadow-grid of your enlightened city.
And now I reach through them – I reach
through the eyes of dreaming sailors,

faces inches from the sweating bulkheads,
blankets drenched in brine and sperm.
Trailing blood across the moon's wake
the ship bore out of Boka Bay.

Trailing sharks, she sailed
for Port Destruction. In Saint Van le Mar,
Jamaica, Bligh's breadfruit trees grew tall.
In Callao on the coast of Peru

geraniums bloomed like sores
against whitewashed walls.
The dock tarts' parrots jabbering
cut-rates in six tongues.

The eroding heartland, inland cordillera
flashing with snow – these the voyager forgets.
His briny eyes
flood with chimerical horizons.

'I would tell you if I could – if I could
remember, I would tell you.
All around us the horizons
are turning air into water

and I can't remember
where the silence ended and speech began,
where vision ended and tears began.
All our promises vanish into thin air.

What I remember are the beaches of that city
whose golden children dance
on broken glass. I remember cold beer
trickling between her breasts as she drank.

But my paper money burned
when she touched it. The ship
clanked up to its bower, the glass towers
of the city burned back there in the sunset glow.'

Cool star foundering in the west.
Coast the dusty colour of lions.
The story navigates by vectors
whose only connection is the story.

The story is told in words
whose only language is the story.
All night the fo'c's'le lamp smokes above the words.
All day the sun counts the hours of the story.

Heave of dark water where something
else turns – the castaway's tongue
clappers like a mission bell.
Unheard his end, and the story's.

Raconteurs in smoky dives
recall his phosphorescent arm
waving in the ship's wake.
Almost gaily. But the ship sailed on.

[1993]

Born in Blenheim in 1946, Ian Wedde spent most of his childhood overseas, first in East Pakistan and then in Britain. Returning to New Zealand in his mid-teens, Wedde attended King's College, Pakuranga, and the University of Auckland, from which he graduated MA (Hons) in English in 1968. While a student at Auckland, he began publishing his poetry in literary journals and in his final year was editor of the *New Zealand Universities Literary Yearbook*.

Upon graduating, Wedde lived for a time in Amman, Jordan, before arriving in London in 1970, where he found work as poetry critic for the *London Magazine*. His first poetry collection, *Homage to Matisse*, appeared in 1971. He returned to New Zealand the following year, taking up a Burns Fellowship at the University of Otago.

Wedde wrote and published poetry and fiction steadily throughout the mid- to late 1970s, gaining a reputation for his willingness to engage with political and theoretical interests in his writing. His output during this period dealt with both local environmental and social issues (*Pathway to the Sea* in 1975 was a long protest-poem addressing the proposed aluminium smelter at Aramoana, on the Otago Peninsula) and the experimental literary movements coming out of the United States, such as the Black Mountain school of poetry. He was also gaining success as a novelist; his first novel – *Dick Seddon's Great Dive* (Dunedin: McIndoe, 1976) – won the New Zealand Book Award for Fiction in 1977. In the 1980s, Wedde co-edited the *Penguin Book of New Zealand Verse* (1985), followed, in 1989, by the *Penguin Book of Contemporary New Zealand Poetry*.

During the mid to late 1980s, Wedde was art critic for the *Evening Post*. This led to a change in focus, with both his professional and critical attention shifting increasingly towards the visual arts. He began working as a curator and in 1994 was appointed concept leader for art at the new national museum of New Zealand, now Te Papa – a position he left in 2004 to return to freelance work.

After producing little poetry during the 1990s, a return to writing in 1999 saw the publication of *The Commonplace Odes* in 2001. This was followed in 2005 by *Three Regrets and a Hymn to Beauty*.

POETRY:

Homage to Matisse. London: Amphedesma Press, 1971.

Made Over: Poems. Auckland: Stephen Chan, 1974.

Earthly: Sonnets for Carlos. Akaroa: Amphedesma Press, 1975.

Pathway to the Sea. Christchurch: Hawk Press, 1975.

Spells for Coming Out. Drawings by Joanna Paul. Auckland: Auckland University Press, 1977.

Castaly. Auckland: Auckland University Press, 1980.

Georgicon. Wellington: Victoria University Press, 1984.

Tales of Gotham City. Auckland: Auckland University Press / Oxford University Press, 1984.

Driving into the Storm: Selected Poems. Auckland: Oxford University Press, 1987.

Tendering. Auckland: Auckland University Press, 1988.

The Drummer. Auckland: Auckland University Press, 1993.

The Commonplace Odes. Auckland: Auckland University Press, 2001.

Three Regrets and a Hymn to Beauty: New Poems. Auckland: Auckland University Press, 2005.

PROSE:

Dick Seddon's Great Dive: A Novel. Dunedin: McIndoe, 1976.

The Shirt Factory and Other Stories. Wellington: Victoria University Press, 1981.

Symmes Hole. Auckland: Penguin, 1986.

Survival Arts. Auckland: Penguin, 1988.

[with Joanna Margaret Paul]. *Wanganui Works: resisting foreclosure*. Wanganui: Sarjeant Gallery, 1989.

[with Peter Black and Peter Ireland]. *Moving Pictures: A Project by Photographer Peter Black, 23 June–29 July 1990, Wellington City Art Gallery*. Wellington: Wellington City Art Gallery, 1990.

How to be Nowhere: Essays and Texts 1971–1994. Wellington: Victoria University Press, 1995.

Making Ends Meet: Essays and Talks, 1992–2004. Wellington: Victoria University Press, 2005.

The Viewing Platform. Auckland: Penguin, 2006.

EDITED:

[with Alan Brunton, Russell Haley and Martin Edmond]. *Spleen*, nos 1–8 (1975–77).

[with Harvey McQueen]. *The Penguin Book of New Zealand Verse*. Introduction and notes by Ian Wedde and Margaret Orbell. Auckland: Penguin, 1985.

[with Miriama Evans and Harvey McQueen]. *The Penguin Book of Contemporary New Zealand Poetry / Nga KupuTuitohu o Aotearoa*. Auckland: Penguin, 1989.

[with Gregory Burke]. *Now See Hear! Art, Language and Translation*. Wellington: Victoria University Press for the Wellington City Art Gallery, 1990.

Fomison, What Shall We Tell Them? Wellington: City Gallery, Wellington, Wellington City Council, 1994.

Dream Collectors: One Hundred Years of Art in New Zealand. Wellington: Te Papa Press, 1998.

FIONA FARRELL (B. 1947)

Anne Brown's Song

[CD 1.31]

I first spread my legs
on a London street
and the shillings came easy
put shoes on my feet
(I've lain on clay
and I've lain on sheet . . .)
And men with rough fingers
have staked out their claims
and gone off up country
no addresses no names.
There's gold in my crannies
there's gold in my crack.
Come miners and diggers
I'm down on my back.
There's a crack in the ceiling
a draught at the door
my back aches my mouth's salt
but there's time for one more.

A nice little bar
with a lamp and a chair
and frosted glass windows
to keep out the air
(there's a crack in the ceiling
a draught at the door)
and no man to empty
his load in my box
no fingers no breathing
no crabs and no pox
and I'll pile up the shillings
to keep in the heat
till I lie in the clay
till I lie in the sheet . . .

[1987]

**Instructions for the Consumption of your Humanitarian
Food Package**

Your package contains:
beans in tomato sauce
beans and tomato vinaigrette
biscuits
fruit pastry
fruit bar
shortbread
peanut butter
strawberry jam
utensils
salt and pepper
a napkin and a match
(Contents of food packages air-dropped in Afghanistan, October 2001.)

Instructions:

1.
Catch your package.
It weighs a kilogram.
It has been dropped from
a great height.
Avoid it as it falls.
A can of beans delivered
at speed can become
a lethal weapon. Any
ordinary thing can kill.

Hide as your package falls.
Bury yourself in the red earth.
The fall comes on like thunder.
Its drops are a heavy rain.

Your package may fall upon a
mine field. It may fall upon
your dinner table, thus scoring

a direct hit. It may fall into
the wrong hands, or it may fall into
the hands of children. It may
fall beyond reach. It may fall
upon deaf ears.

2.

Open your humanitarian package
with care. Do not spill its contents on
stony ground. Do not expose its
contents to the scrutiny of sunlight, nor
store it at temperatures below freezing.
Consume immediately, using the knife
and fork provided and spreading your
napkin so that it will catch every crumb.
Wash your hands on the completion of
your meal, using any available water.
Dispose of all wrappings in a manner
which acknowledges the beauty of this
red earth. Give thanks to the force that
sends you food and instruction
from thin air.

3.

There is no recommended sequence
for the consumption of your humanitarian
package. You live in a free world. You
can set a fire with your match. You
can light a candle. You can sharpen
your utensils, or use them to spread jam
on your beans. You can eat this food in
any order and in any combination. You
can add peanut butter to the vinaigrette
or eat shortbread with salt and pepper.
It makes no difference. Should your
belly swell and split like a seedhead
you will see that all food dissolves in
the acids natural to the human stomach.

We do recommend, however, that you
eat fast. There is food for only one day.
There is food for only 35,000 and 6
million are waiting. We recommend
that you dispense with ceremony.
Grab.
Eat while you can.

4.
When they look out at daybreak
they see that the thorn bushes are
coated in sticky substances. The
children of the wilderness are afraid,
not knowing if this be the fruit of good
or evil. But hunger forces its own solution.
They taste, they lick their fingers. They
perch by the bushes like the small brown
birds who fly in flocks, nesting where they can.
They have no proper names because they
are so common, these sparrow children.
They are so many that their fall cannot
be marked from any distance.

They swarm out at daybreak
thousands of them
to strip the bushes,
taking sweet stuff from strangers.

[2002]

Fiona Farrell was born in Oamaru and educated in Otago and Toronto, where she wrote
her thesis on T. S. Eliot and poetic drama. Her publications include three collections of
poetry (*Cutting Out* in 1987, *The Inhabited Initial* in 1999 and the newly published *Pop-
Up Book of Invasions*), two collections of short stories (*The Rock Garden*, 1989, and *Light
Readings*, 2001) and five novels: *The Skinny Louie Book*, 1992, winner of the New Zealand
Book Award for Fiction in 1993; *Six Clever Girls Who Became Famous Women*, 1996; *The
Hopeful Traveller*, 2002; *Book Book*, 2004; and, most recently, *Mr Allbones' Ferrets*. Both *The
Hopeful Traveller* and *Book Book* were shortlisted for the Montana New Zealand Book

Awards. She was writer in residence at Canterbury University in 1992 and received the Katherine Mansfield Fellowship to Menton, France in 1995. She also participated in New Zealand Book Council Words on Wheels tours in 1993, 1997 and 2001. Her poems and stories have been widely anthologised. She has appeared at several festivals, including the Edinburgh Festival and the Vancouver International Writers and Readers Festival in 2006.

POETRY:
Cutting Out. Auckland: Auckland University Press, 1987.
The Inhabited Initial. Auckland: Auckland University Press, 1999.
The Pop-Up Book of Invasions. Auckland: Auckland University Press, 2007.

PROSE:
The Rock Garden: Stories. Auckland: Auckland University Press, 1989.
The Skinny Louie Book. Auckland: Penguin New Zealand, 1992.
Six Clever Girls Who Became Famous Women. Auckland: Penguin New Zealand, 1996.
Light Readings: Stories. Auckland: Vintage, 2001.
The Hopeful Traveller. Auckland: Vintage, 2002.
Book Book. Auckland: Vintage, 2004.
Mr Allbones' Ferrets. Auckland: Vintage, 2007.

KERI HULME (B. 1947)

[CD I.33] *from* **Fisher in an Autumn Tide**

bubbles

bubbles . . .

from the winter-rusted willows
from the old bone in the shallows
from the watching shadow

that could be a fish:

eyes which look through unnatural windows
mistake the obvious, see hopeful matter where
there is no warrant

and light strikes me so hard now.
an unwary glance   see! sunglint
                     see! a match struck in the dark
                     see! a torch flick
they blind, I see nothing except that obscuring flare
greenish overwhelming all the world out there

        – one of my brothers says Don't you wish we could
        wake up one morning
just *one* morning and *see?*
See around us?
See what waits?
See where we're going?

                Yeah

We all have interesting feet in my family.
Our toes cringe as soon as we get out of bed.
They would sigh if they could.

Instead, with scarred & practised tentativity
they feel their way into the day:
groping is our mode of being
fingering guessing where the solid is listening
with myopes' too-sharp ears for the way.

I have tried to hear fish.
Wiser, today I flick a fly to the shadow by the trailing willow
split shot clips the water there is no splash

nothing happens.

A purist would say Kaitoa, good job, serve you right
sneering the while at the little baitcaster, pistol-grip rod and
dinky svelte-profiled teardrop reel, sneering at the contemptible
2 k nylon, the kind that does not throw any reflection show
any kind of light; sneering at – Hey! but I tied that straggly black spider
        myself, mate,
and underwater it must look like tucker because it's fooled and killed
two fish to date –

that's all I'm doing today, pothunting not practising any high form of
The Art, The Game, The Way.
I'm fishing for my stomach's sake and the keener for it.

To my mind, you're either playing – so, call it sport
(or call it fishtorture as an animal-rights cousin of mine does if you're so
        inclined;
neither upsets me nor enlightens me, having figured out early that there are
        two sides in every
game, whether you're a party on an ancient ball court or having fun by
        yourself or
stumbling around life)
but basically you're playing or
you're there to catch food.

I'm here, having at shadows
which don't move.

Why has nobody invented a fishscope for us myopes?
Oh yes, I've tried binoculars. They make the indistinct
clearly indistinct, wobble the world alarmingly and magnify sunglints
to sear so hard that's it for the day.
And as for anything else, polarised fishing-specs and things
– I'm the one wearing sunglasses to the bonfire
      at midnight –

I need a fish-spotting device
they used to called them cormorants, shags in our parlance,
equip them with a choker and retrieval-string and
send 'em out for lunch.

The shag on the stump over there
spreads its wings wider, and sneers.
The sunlight beams
O well, I'll keep on fishing blind then

                  and a fin fingers
                  a fin fingers my line

The hours drift by before I realise they've evanesced.
Days so, years, and with them the might-have-beens
that died, that went beyond regret, returning only as hard memory
      – I mean solid, steely, pinching the mind suddenly
as this tool pinches the hook,
forceps relocated from a city A & E one tense evening – they clattered
on the floor and were ignored and I absently
picked them up from the fringe of things and toyed with them and
tucked them in a pocket.
How do you explain such petty forgetful theft? So
attached to a black reelup, pinned to my beltpouch, they no longer
clamp arteries, just hooks, tiny hooks, this hook I've just defanged and now
slip out: she lies stunned still.
a hen trout: she had danced and fought up the riff of water
for twenty minutes sleek power in the dying sun
until drawn to the dubious safety of my net. She weighs
about three pounds I think but I've already killed a heavier jack

and she fought so well.

He'll feed the three of us – holding her gill-on to the current moving

her gently forward a little forward into the blind water.

Her fins flicker wearily, she weaves slowly off, but she doesn't bleed and

she'll do. I think, she'll do.

Live, that is.

There was a lot of blood that evening in the A & E, enough to make skilled

    fingers slippery

and instruments skate away. They should practise on fish maybe,

for the grip I mean. Then again, that's only if I want to hold to kill.

That hen, lost in the brown distance, felt the wet cotton gloves but never suf-

    fered

pressure or the flame of my flesh – as for other

suffering, who can tell? I can't hear fish scream either.

The forceps tuck back against my belt.

Enough for this evening, I think.

[2004]

Born in Christchurch, Keri Hulme was educated at North Brighton Primary and Aranui High Schools. After some study at Canterbury University, she worked in the Motueka tobacco fields and subsequently tried a number of different occupations while writing her first stories and poems.

Hulme's first collection of poems, *The Silence Between (Moeraki Conversations),* was published in 1982. Her homage to Moeraki ('my turangawaewae ngakau') and Okarito appeared in *Homeplaces* (1989) and another collection of poems, *Strands,* was published in 1992.

In 1985, while she was writer in residence at the University of Canterbury, her novel *the bone people* won the Booker Prize, an event which catapulted her to world fame.

She now lives, works, paints (and catches whitebait) in the tiny South Westland settlement of Okarito. Her most recent published work is *Stonefish* (2004).

POETRY:

Coast Voices. Ed. Roger Ewer. Greymouth: Walden Books, 1979.

Silences Between (Moeraki Conversations). Auckland: Auckland University Press / Oxford University Press, 1982.

Strands. Auckland: Auckland University Press, 1992.

PROSE:

the bone people. Wellington: Spiral, 1983; Auckland: Spiral: Hodder & Stoughton, 1985; London: Pan, 1986; Baton Rouge: Louisiana State University Press, 2005.

Lost Possessions. Wellington: Victoria University Press, 1985.

The Windeater / Te Kaihau. Wellington: Victoria University Press, 1986.

Homeplaces: Three Coasts of the South Island. With Robin Morrison. Auckland: Hodder & Stoughton, 1989.

Hokitika Handmade. Photographs by Julia Brooke-White. Hokitika: Hokitika Craft Gallery Co-operative, 1999.

Stonefish. Wellington: Huia Publishers, 2004.

MURRAY EDMOND (B. 1949)

Voyager

[CD 1.34]

after Apollinaire

    To have a vision, you must leave home – Alan Brunton

open this door where I knock while weeping

the dunes of Kanaka the deserts of Niger
the desalination plants of Kuwait
the fish-markets of Dakar

life is variable
as is also the tidal rip at Whaainga-roa

LIGHT IN THE STOMACH LIGHT IN THE SPIRIT
the billboard read
and I looked for you there
standing among long grass
and discarded plastic
as if you were in a piece of street theatre
but you were not there

you pay your regards to a bank of clouds which drops
low to the horizon
along with an orphaned tramp steamer heading out into
overheated futures

the reefs of Australia the villages of Mali
the 2000 islands of the city of Stockholm

and of all these regrets and all these repentances
can you remember
the waves the flying fish the flowers on the water

across the night water candles in small tents fire
flies and crackle of frogs
on the sound system
hidden in the bulrushes
but you were not there

the bird-carvings of Peru the rivers of France the
icebergs of Tierra del Fuego
the gypsies of Venice
the refugee camp near Tirana
the patchwork of carpets at Marrakech

one night it was the sea
and the rivers spread themselves out

 I remember it I remember it always

in the park in the summer evening a pianist played
what had been once revolutionary dances
by the famous composer
but it was not you

those girls from the Ukraine
or was it Belarus
in the old town square
who stood so poorly and were dressed like shopgirls
and sang as though they would tear open the fabric of the night
the tears of things and the things of tears
was this something you had organised

one evening I came to a sad hotel
in the vicinity of Luxembourg
in the depths of my room a Christ was flying
someone had a ferret
someone else had a porcupine
we played cards together
and you had forgotten me

the flooded plains of Bengal the algae farms of Bali
the uranium mines of Kakadu National Park the
sandbanks of Bolivar
the log rafts of the Amazon

here's a question
do you remember the long orphanage of trains
the towns we crossed which all day went spinning round
and at night they vomited the sun
o sailors o sombre women and you comrades of mine
do you remember any of it

for a moment I thought the beggar on crutches in the tram
a real piece of Peachum fancy dress
who was such a good actor must have been
but he wasn't

the vats of the dyers of Fez
the wheatfields of Rajasthan
the fjords of Norway the volcanoes
and the mineral forests of Madagascar
and the bales of cotton of the Ivory Coast
where the worker is lying back and taking his rest

two sailors who never quit each other
two sailors who never spoke
that young one died
and the body washed up on the shore

beloved comrades
sound of electric trains song of generators
the butcher's van going from door to door
in the streets of Leningrad
the regiment in the numberless streets
the cavalcade of bridges
shining drunken nights
the cities I have seen live the lives of crazy women

the bus reeked of alcohol I opened the bag of photos
and looked inside
but no no
not there

the place where wild strawberries grow
one of the heart-breaking accumulations of landscape
the cypresses projected their shadows under the moon
listening to the night at the end of summer
a languorous bird and one in a constant state of irritation
and the sound of the broad black river running by
despite the dead carried on the flood towards the estuary
every look every look of every eye
the banks were silent grassy deserts
and in the other direction the mountain was shining

greenhouses north of the Arctic Circle alight day and night
plastic tents for strawberries on the Costa Brava
the Tiergarten in Berlin the rows of discarded B52s
in the David Monmouth Air Force Base near Tucson Arizona
lying asleep waiting to be stripped of their parts

there was a crowd around the clown
who held a yellow skeleton
dangling from a stick
on the Ramblas
and I looked among the faces of the crowd
and there stood one with an ironic lean
and I thought for a moment it was

against the mountainside
with no other sight or sound
of any living thing
shadows slipped across the mountainside
vivacious shadows
some in profile
some turned their faces to stare
they carried their weapons
held out in front like scripts

scrolled down through the paragraphs of text
the messages
the vocabulary was stentorian and elliptical
so it could have been
but no

the shadows came and went in size
pulsing smaller pulsing larger
shapes of men with beards who wept humanly
step by step they crossed the shining mountain
a puppet play

the graveyard of tanks in the desert near Al-Jahrah
the abandoned city of Pripiat near Chernobyl
the bagel shops of Manhattan
the expanding shores and shrinking waters of the Aral Sea
splintered corals of Mururoa
water hyacinths on the Nile
where a boat is trapped in their foliage
the Boat of a Million Years
clouds of flamingos over Lake Nukuru
the red earth of Siena
the piazza at carnival

look at the photographs
the day the bee fell in the fire
remember
you were there
at the end of summer

two sailors who never quit each other
the older one carried a chain around the neck
the younger was braiding blond hair into dreads

open this door where I knock while weeping

as is the rip tide at Whaainga-roa

Warsaw, July 2002

Murray Edmond was born in Hamilton in 1949. He was educated at the University of Auckland (1968–71), where he edited two issues of *The Word is Freed* and worked as literary editor for *Craccum*, the student newspaper.

In the 1970s and 1980s he worked as an actor, writer and director for various companies – the Living Theatre Troupe, Beggar's Bag Theatre, Theatre Action, The Half Moon Theatre (London), Town and Country Players and the Mercury Theatre.

His dramaturgy includes David Geary's *Lovelock's Dream Run*, Jacob Rajan and Justin Lewis's *Krishnan's Dairy*, *The Candlestickmaker and The Pickle King*, Toa Fraser's *No. 2* and *Paradise*, and Witi Ihimaera's *Woman Far Walking*.

He is the author of ten books of poetry and the editor of three anthologies. The most recent of these are, respectively, *Fool Moon*, with photographs by Joanna Forsberg (2005), and *Big Smoke: New Zealand Poems 1960–1975* (2000) with Alan Brunton and Michele Leggott.

His doctoral thesis was a history of New Zealand experimental theatre from 1962 to 1982 entitled *Old Comrades of the Future*. At present he teaches drama, theatre and poetry in the English department at the University of Auckland.

POETRY:

Entering the Eye. Dunedin: Caveman Press, 1973.
Patchwork: Poems. Wellington: Hawk Press, 1978.
End Wall: Poems. Auckland: Oxford University Press, 1981.
Letters and Paragraphs. Christchurch: Caxton Press, 1987.
[with Keith Sinclair and C. K. Stead]. *Three Poems for Kendrick Smithyman*. Auckland: Department of English, Auckland University Press, 1987.
From the Word Go. Auckland: Auckland University Press, 1992.
The Switch. Auckland: Auckland University Press, 1994.
Names/Manes. Artist's Chapbook with Anna Miles, 1996.
Laminations. Auckland: Auckland University Press, 2000.
A Piece of Work. Kaneohe, Hawaii: Tinfish, 2002.
Fool Moon. Photographs by Joanna Forsberg. Auckland: Auckland University Press, 2004.

PROSE:

Noh Business. Berkeley: Atelos, 2005.

EDITED:

The Word is Freed, nos 3–4 (1970–71).
[with Mary Paul]. *The New Poets: Initiatives in New Zealand Poetry*. Wellington: Port Nicholson Press, 1987.
[with Alan Brunton and Michele Leggott]. *Big Smoke: New Zealand Poems 1960–1975*. Auckland: Auckland University Press, 2000.
[with Chang Hua and John Tranter]. *Australia New Zealand Anthology of Poetry*. Peking, 1993.
Ka Mate Ka Ora: A New Zealand Journal of Poetry and Poetics. Bi-annual. First issue December 2005. www.nzepc.auckland.ac.nz/kmko/index.asp.

JAN KEMP (B. 1949)

Against the softness of woman [CD 1.35]

Vagrant woman pawn your Piscean flood,
don't wave your flower, keep your blood
dry as the gaze behind your eye:
let the resilient bitch rise
in the belly of your skies
& front it without
your usual vacillation.

You were born to fit him,
to be his lay, his lie,
his way to run his way;
when he has pared down his spare image
don't try to catch him
you'll catch yourself –

don't let the quick spring flow
hide it behind: cut your
lip-service, your idolatry;
he has bared himself translucent
like the rings of honesty;
don't be the dry pip between his petals
he will spit you out –

when you are sunk tight on the pain
let his singularity teach you:
soften your gall, it wanes thin
held in the light – transparency
holds no mystery; become like him
wear your other heart on your other sleeve,
keep this one boned down fine.

Auckland, June 1971

Jousting

She's so glad she never said never to his
when are we going to have an affair? Instead
(knowing he wouldn't) she said *when you take
the same emotional risk I would I will*
and he whistled in even more admiration
but of the kind that (surprise!) showed
she'd outwitted him. She was so young then
she told his best mate who, after a consoling
drink, tried the same number (married too of course)
& wouldn't take Plato's way – *it's lovers or not, get it?*
haranguing her between St. Helier's Bay fountain
the Berkeley, Harris coffee shop & the seawall –
and try as she did to talk history, philosophy to
testosterone incarnate, he wouldn't give in –
so that was friendship forever exempted.
No wonder she went overseas. But men
here were like that then except for
Hermes, who ran along the waterfront
straight off the sea, blond, sandals streaming –
he's the one held her till kingdom come
who never did nor ever tried. Because
of that how she still favours him.

[2006]

The sky's enormous jug

Swathed in a bed sheet
her Egyptian lover
lies still as a sarcophagus.

She lies beside her Pharaoh
a queen, holding ankh
& crook in crossed hands.

The curtain lifts, the sail
of their *felucca*. Together they
glide onto the Nile of night.

He sleeps. She watches
teeming stars pour onto their bed
from the sky's enormous jug.

Her breasts still tingle.
This, an apricot season
– *bukra fi el mishmish* –

slipped in between the lines
that say we live we die.

[2001]

Sailing boats   [CD 1.38]

Watch from the deck
the origami Ps
& optimist Qs
slip off
the tide's tongue

bob out
into the bay –
wayang kulit
gone to sea

white napkins
nodding together
on a pulled
turquoise cloth.

[2006]

'Bukra fi el mishmish' is an Egyptian quip, Arabic for 'tomorrow in the time of the apricots',
meaning you postpone the act so that it will never happen *or* that it will happen in a dream time.
'Wayang kulit' are Indonesian shadow puppets.

'Love is a babe . . .'

William Shakespeare, Sonnet 115

I was a babe of eighteen when I fell –
twice Beatrice's age when Dante saw her.

I stood on a bridge between innocence
& knowledge – babes are like that –

nonchalant, petrified & full of love.
You looked up at the bridge, saw me,

stopped & I knew you knew in a sun flash
as Beatrice did. It chokes me still.

The world spins from under my hands.
Palms on my cheeks. I cannot hide.

I am six nines old. Beatus, it grows
& I carry it as Will said I would.

[2006]

Born in Hamilton 1949, Jan Kemp has a BA and an MA (Hons) in English from the
University of Auckland, a Diploma of Teaching (Auckland Teacher's College), an RSA
TEFL Certificate (British Council, Hong Kong) and the PNDS and Zwischenprüfung
from the J. W. Goethe-Universität, Frankfurt. After graduation she lived and taught at
various universities for many years in the South Pacific, Canada, Asia and Germany,
including the universities of Papua New Guinea, Hong Kong, East Asia at Macau, the
National University of Singapore and J. W. Goethe-Universtät, Frankfurt am Main.
She studied German and Italian literature in Frankfurt for five years until her return
home to live in Torbay on Auckland's North Shore in late 1999, with her husband Dieter
Riemenschneider.
     She first published and performed as a *Freed* poet in the late 1960s and was the only
woman contributor to *The Young New Zealand Poets* anthology in 1973. She was co-collec-
tor of the Waiata Archive and in 1974 co-editor with Jonathan Lamb and Alan Smythe of
Waiata Recordings three-LP album *New Zealand Poets Read Their Work*. In 1979 she toured
New Zealand with Alistair Campbell, Sam Hunt and Hone Tuwhare on the NZUSA

'Gang of Four' poets tour and was in the New Zealand contingent at the South Pacific Festival of Arts in Port Moresby, Papua New Guinea, in 1980. Since returning to live in New Zealand in 1999, she has taken part in the New Zealand Book Council's Words on Wheels tour of the Waikato (with Michael King, Peter Wells and others) and New Zealand Poetry Society's Northern Lights tour (both in 2002). She was the first New Zealand poet to be granted a writer-in-residency at the Château de Lavigny, Switzerland, 2006.

In the Queen's Birthday Honours 2005 she was awarded an MNZM for services to literature.

POETRY:
Against the Softness of Woman. Dunedin: Caveman Press, 1976.
Diamonds and Gravel. Wellington: Hampson Hunt, 1979.
[with Hone Tuwhare, Sam Hunt and Alistair Campbell]. *4 New Zealand Poets: New Zealand Tour, Winter 1979*. Wellington: New Zealand Students' Arts Council, 1979.
Ice-Breaker Poems. Auckland: Printed by Coal-Black Press, 1980.
Five Poems. Singapore: National Museum Art Gallery, 1988.
The Other Hemisphere: Poems. Washington, DC: Three Continents Press, 1991; Springwood, NSW: Butterfly Books, 1991.
Europa: For Female Voice and Piano. Music by Nicholas Routley; texts by Ovid and Jan Kemp. Grosvenor Place, NSW: Australian Music Centre, 1999.
Only One Angel: Poems. Dunedin: University of Otago Press, 2001.
The Sky's Enormous Jug: Love Poems. Auckland: Puriri Press, 2001.
[with Lynda Chanwai-Earle and Glenn Colquhoun]. *Northern Lights: The New Zealand Poetry Society Presents Three Northern Poets to Light up our Southern Skies*. Christchurch: Firebrand in association with the New Zealand Poetry Society, 2002.
Dante's Heaven. Auckland: Puriri Press, 2006.

EDITED:
[with Jonathan Lamb and Alan Smythe]. *New Zealand Poets Read Their Work* and *New Zealand Poets Read Their Work for Children* [3 LPs]. Auckland: Waiata Recordings, 1974.
[with Jack Ross]. *Classic New Zealand Poets in Performance* [book and CDs]. Auckland: Auckland University Press, 2006.

CILLA MCQUEEN (B. 1949)

[CD 1.40] **Living Here**

Well you'd have to remember this place
is just one big city with 3 million people with
a little flock of sheep each so we're all sort of
shepherds
           little human centres each within an outer
circle of sheep around us like a ring of
covered wagons   we all know we'll probably
be safe when the Indians finally come
down from the hills   (comfortable to live
in the Safest Place in the World)
                        sheep being
very thick and made of wool and leather
being a very effective shield as ancient
soldiers would agree.
             And you can also
sit on them of course and wear them and eat them
so after all we are lucky to have these
sheep in abundance   they might
have been hedgehogs –
             Then we'd all be
used to hedgehogs and clothed in prickles
rather than fluff
          and the little sheep would
come out sometimes at night under the moon
and we'd leave them saucers of milk
                  and feel sad
seeing them squashed on the road
Well anyway here we are with all this
cushioning in the biggest city in the world
its suburbs strung out in a long line
and the civic centre at the bottom of
Cook Strait   some of them Hill Suburbs

and some Flat Suburbs and some more prosperous
than others
        some with a climate that embarrasses
them and a tendency to grow strange small fruit
some temperate and leafy   whose hot streets lull
So here we are again in the biggest
safest city in the world   all strung out
over 1500 miles one way   and a little bit
the other
      each in his woolly protection
so sometimes it's difficult to see out
the eyes   let alone call to each other
which is the reason for the loneliness some
of us feel
      and for our particular relations
with the landscape   that we trample
or stroke with our toes or eat or lick
tenderly or pull apart
        and love   like an
old familiar lover who fits us
curve to curve   and hate because it
knows us and knows our weakness
We're calling fiercely to each other
through the muffled spaces   grateful for
any wrist-brush
       cut of mind or touch of music,
lightning in the intimate weather of the soul.

[1982]

Fuse

The road winds back in time
as we drive down the Otago Peninsula
to Te Rauone. It is a visit,
a kind of unveiling — in my mind
the meeting house at Otakou,
Weller's rock, the fishing wharf,
and around the corner a wooden house
with an orange roof and a pohutukawa tree.

A long stone wall runs beside the road
from the head of the harbour
all the way along the peninsula northwards,
a blue-black drystone wall
built by the Maori prisoners from Parihaka.
This wall runs back in time —
in one of these small bays
you might see soldiers at ease under a tree
toss crumbs to seagulls
while they watch the Taranaki men break rock.

Fire springs from the curved steel pick;
anger drives deep inside the lizard wall
that twists through torn fields of their sleep
in stone cells cut in the cliff
where clay walls sweat like dying men.
The scarred moon blesses the hands of whanau
that twine at the bars like roots.
Te Whiti's words, white feathers, fill the darkness.
A candle, a murmur of prayer.
At night the iron-barred window sings.

The lizard flickers its tongue
as we pass the fishing wharf, the small boats,
and round the corner — there is Te Rauone beach,
the sandhills, seagrass, Taiaroa Head beyond,
the seabirds, the channel, Aramoana —

only there is no house
and in the ground no trace of ash,
just soft green lupins,
growing in clean sand,
red stars on the pohutukawa.

Loss of possessions is a kind of freedom;
loss of the land is exile.
The pickaxes strike fire.
The wall runs back towards the city,
a fuse slow-burning through the generations
ready to flare; past time nearly visible
behind the surface of this sunny day,
the harbour sparkling — on the car radio, news
of an unarmed Maori man
shot dead by the police last night, in Waitara.

May 2000

Cilla McQueen was born in 1949 in Birmingham, England, and is now a New Zealand citizen. She graduated from Otago University with a first-class MA Hons in 1971. She works as a poet, teacher and artist.

In 1983 she won the New Zealand Book Award for Poetry for *Homing In*, as well as the PEN/Jessie Mackay Award for Best First Book of Poetry. In 1985–86 she was the Robert Burns Fellow at Otago University and held a Goethe Institut Scholarship in Berlin in 1988. In 1989 she again won the New Zealand Book Award for Poetry for *Benzina* and yet again in 1991 for *Berlin Diary*.

She now lives in Bluff, and was one of the organisers of the nzepc Bluff poetry symposium in 2006, with Michele Leggott and David Howard.

POETRY:
Homing In. Dunedin: McIndoe, 1982.
Anti Gravity. Dunedin: McIndoe, 1984.
Wild Sweets. Dunedin: McIndoe, 1986.
Benzina. Dunedin: McIndoe, 1988.
[with David Farquhar]. *Three Cilla McQueen Songs: Mezzo-soprano/Baritone and Piano*.
    Wellington: Wai-te-ata Press, 1988.
[with Alistair Macdougall]. *Otherwise* [sound recording]. Dunedin: Rowan, 1989.
Berlin Diary. Dunedin: McIndoe, 1990.

Crīk'ey: New and Selected Poems 1978–1994. Dunedin: McIndoe, 1994.

Markings: Poems and Drawings. Dunedin: University of Otago Press, 2000.

Parihaka: The Art of Passive Resistance [sound recording]. Wellington: Morrison Music Trust, 2000.

Axis: Poems and Drawings. Dunedin: University of Otago Press, 2001.

Soundings: Poems and Drawings. Dunedin: University of Otago Press, 2002.

Fire-penny. Dunedin: University of Otago Press, 2005.

A Wind Harp: Poems by Cilla McQueen [sound recording]. Dunedin: University of Otago, 2006.

BOB ORR (B. 1949)

The X [CD 2.1]

Across the rd
the tobacconist
sits outside in the sun
most of the time & knows
I study him / I sit on
the bed u shaped with
our weight at midday
the drunk
with his smashed guitar
wants a dollar
for a black bottle of wine
in the kitchen someone shoots
marmite / beneath the stairs
a stranger makes out he's Christ
every day they both
get worse / I count the atoms
in the wall / I'm leaving soon
with my barefooted heart

[1971]

A Country Shaped like a Butterfly's Wing

Beneath this giant pohutukawa
the cares of the world seem to cease.
Concrete steps zigzag from the street to a sandy beach
where rusty boat sheds stand on stilts
and women whose bodies are shaped like gourds
walk miraculously into and out of the sea.
You talk but I only half listen . . . some minutes since
you left me at a bay where the sun like a sword
plunges between the horns of blue breakers.
Beneath this summer's slow travelling clouds
I am reminded that we both have ancestors
who once upon a time sailed across the world's biggest oceans.
In their webs of latitude and longitude
like fishermen flinging a net
they caught this solitary planet
floating in blue space like a chrysalis.
Thank you for bringing me here
where the roots of a pohutukawa
like handrails lead down a cliff –
where the flight of seagulls is as eternal as hunger is.
Perhaps we should be like those Persians
beneath a swaying branch with a loaf of bread and a bottle of wine –
watch clouds like caravans sauntering across the horizon.
Should we stay here until the night has fallen into the sea –
in the morning council workers
would find the imprint of our bodies
close together on a quilt of leaves.
I talk but you only half listen
as we lie beneath this tree
through whose branches life is whispering.
Its roots run right through the spicy earth to Spain.
As we lie beneath blossoms tinged with Garcia Lorca's blood
do you dream of a country shaped like a butterfly's wing?

[2002]

Ballad of the Great South Rd

[CD 2.3]

My dad drove red herds of cattle
up the Great South Road

between railway track
and river bank

following the river's flow
following each wide curve

many years
ago.

A chestnut horse he rode
my dad

when he was just
a farm boy from the Waikato.

The horse
ended up at a knacker's sale

but in the shed
the saddle and the bridle

are tied with a piece of hay bale twine
to the end of a rusty nail.

I dream of a horse
that canters up to the gate

dispersing
clouds of sandflies

and presses its head
to my dad's head

as if to say
just one more ride.

[2002]

Eternity

Eternity is the traffic lights at Huntly –
before they change from red to green
I am lost in the enchantment of an ancient entertainment.
A wraith-like old wooden two-storey hotel
a war memorial hall with a padlocked front door
the sour taste on my tongue of a dust and diesel railway station
miners' cottages pale as mushrooms in the mist
a seesaw in the playground of a primary school
like scales that tilt towards injustice –
all become fantastical and floating
like some surreal craft now cast adrift by phantom boatmen.
Tilted on the river's broad traverse
the topsy-turvy of its history
down a surface cross threaded and riddled with mysteries
wide from its flashing underbelly
its streetlights like a gorse bloom's yellow carnival
through coal black waters voyaging this corridor of stars.
Do I merely chance to catch a glimpse of Mum and Dad
after a day out at the races
waltzing on the balcony of the Waipa Hotel –
Dad with his pockets full of fancy
the town's wake of champagne corks and ribbons
Mum laughing as he murmurs something?
All these years later in a midsummer night's dream
as I'm saying hullo and saying goodbye to them
waiting at the traffic lights as Huntly floats downstream.

[2002]

The son of a Waikato farming family, Bob Orr was born in Hamilton in 1949, where he attended St Paul's Collegiate. After moving to Auckland, he enrolled briefly at the University of Auckland (1967) and became prominent among the poets associated with the Auckland University Literary Society's magazine *Freed* in the early 1970s. He lives in Auckland, where he works as a boatman.

Orr has published six collections of his poetry. In addition, his poems have been anthologised in *The Young New Zealand Poets* (1973); *The Penguin Book of New Zealand Verse* (1985); *The Penguin Book of Contemporary New Zealand Poetry* (1989); and *An Anthology of New Zealand Poetry in English* (1997).

POETRY:

Blue Footpaths. London: Amphedesma Press, 1971.

Poems for Moira. Wellington: Hawk Press, 1979.

Cargo. Wellington: Voice Press, 1983.

Red Trees. Auckland: Auckland University Press / Oxford University Press / Silverfish, 1985.

Breeze. Auckland: Auckland University Press, 1991.

Valparaiso. Auckland: Auckland University Press, 2002.

GEOFF COCHRANE (B. 1951)

[CD 2.5] **Spindrift Sunday**

There are, of course, the children
as rowdy as dwarves,
a beloved wife whose hair
smells of graphite and sebum.

But you leave the sodden lawn
and burdened hollyhocks
to drive into the country.
You know a man who butchers cars
in a disused abattoir.

Poplars. Idle signals. Silent bells.
Leaving is like arriving.
The town ends in dandelions and silos;
the rain drifts in like seed.

[1999]

[CD 2.6] **1988**

My casement opens upon
viridian lushness,
the drenched and viridescent paradise
of Central Park

Someone posts me a hunk of faecal matter

When the pot on the stove boils dry,
an egg bursts
its flesh begins to roast
a can of minestrone explodes

Big Jim bathes and powders,
puts on his flash hibiscus shirt
and dies without a sound
seated upright in his chair

In the absence of a Bible,
the sergeant makes us swear
on the Big Book of AA

The undertaker's intrigued
by the shape-of-a-heater hole
burned through the floor

Befriend me, Robert Lowell

Stay me with flagons, Stanley Moss

[2001]

Zigzags

[CD 2.7]

And what was the city to us
if not a sweet protracted sacrament?
As innocent as grunts we headed out
determined to know the foul and fair of it,

its driven rain & rosy overcast
its murky brass & panes of clouded ice
its lights imprisoned by steel grilles
its altars knobby with bluebells & snails

its Roxies / Ferris wheels / recumbent lions
its small octagonal tiles of black and white
its Chinese restaurants with tanks of carp
its pantographs & blue cascades of sparks
its swimming pools of blood & fiery cloud

And oh to drink those mists & foggy glares,
to feed one's living face to that dark conflagration
streaming ever blackly in upon itself,
to that smooth rapid vortex of combustion
streaming ever blackly in upon itself,
and oh to merge one's own pluvial heart
with greenish dawn & aqueous rainbow

As swart & lean as soldiers we took on
vodka / acid / Mandrax / tequila / smack
drowned in shallow puddles of neon and oil
conferred with fallen anaesthetists
overdosed suavely in purple bedrooms
jumped in flapping coats from viaducts
discharged our wonky liquorice shotguns
saluted the golden breast of the Lizard King
froze to death in sanctifying snows of white noise

(An X-ray of a flea-pit in the badlands
revealed the fuzzy souls of methylated cops

Because I was a poet people died
Because I was a poet, people died

[2001]

[CD 2.8] **Atlantis**

It rains and rains.
I discover an old edition of Leonard Cohen,
sweet musty poems from the Sixties
(I'll always remember a certain kitchen).

It rains and rains but everyone is snug,
perfectly serene and capable,
at home on the streets.

GEOFF COCHRANE

Lured by sleet and spume,
man and woman waltz
out of the restaurant and onto the wharf.

The dancer lifts his heel.

A trawler roosts on a green swell.

Parts of the island are disappearing.

[2001]

Geoff Cochrane was born in 1951 in Island Bay, Wellington, and educated at St Patrick's College, Cambridge Terrace. His first books were private-press productions; his current publishers are Thumbprint Press and Victoria University Press. He has contributed verse and stories to *JAAM*, *Takahe*, *PRINTOUT*, the *New Zealand Listener*, *Best New Zealand Poems*, *Landfall* and *Sport*. His poems appear in many recent anthologies.

POETRY:
Images of Midnight City. Hauraki Press, 1976.
The Sea the Landsman Knows. Wellington: Voice Press, 1980.
Taming the Smoke. Wellington: Grape Press, 1983.
Kandinsky's Mirror. Wellington: Rat Island Press, 1989.
Aztec Noon. Wellington: Victoria University Press, 1992.
Into India. Wellington: Victoria University Press, 1999.
Acetylene. Wellington: Victoria University Press, 2001.
Nine Poems. Wellington: Fernbank Studio, 2002.
Vanilla Wine. Wellington: Victoria University Press, 2003.
Hypnic Jerks. Wellington: Victoria University Press, 2005.

PROSE:
Tin Nimbus. Wellington: Victoria University Press, 1995.
Blood. Wellington: Victoria University Press, 1997.
Brindle Embers. Wellington: Thumbprint Press, 2002.
White Nights. Wellington: Thumbprint Press, 2004.

BILL SEWELL (1951–2003)

[CD 2.9]   **Jahrhundertwende**

Always saying goodbye, or goodnight; never quite
with us, never quite gone; balancing on the final
moment. For it's easier somehow to be always
leaving, autumnal and crepuscular, half-season,
half-light.
         So you can linger if you wish
in a deckchair on the Lido, watch the sunset,
see the century out. You can pack and
unpack your bags, and ignore the warnings
that, over the water, the plague is seeping
along the streets.
                 Whatever might be fading
before your eyes: the boy with rotten teeth,
the madman's castle, the corroding forest,
the park they say is dead, you will always look
back in blindness and make it beautiful.

[1986]

[CD 2.10]   **Riversdale**

There are towns in the South
you wouldn't dip your head-
lights for: the hotel,
the store, the service station

and they're gone, a quick
hiatus on the plain.
Whatever your thirst
it must stay unquenched;

for even the Mobil man
is not so obliging
he'll stand to attention
all night. And whatever lights

still let on that anyone's
at home, gaze inwards
incommunicado.
                    The dark
and the distance must

still be kept out
and above all you Northerners,
who talk as fast
as you drive; who rap

on the counter expecting
instant service. Who think
that the South can be subdued
in a single transit.

[2001]

Breaking the quiet   [CD 2.11]

Nobody was there
to hear the impact
but the quiet
that came after
would have been immense –

before the skuas
scenting the news
came skidding out of the mist
before the breeze
lifted to a whistle –

quieter than light
percolating
through the ice
quieter than
the prickling of nerves

quieter than snow
its gentle entrance
quieter than sleep
quieter even than
the hissing of time.

The approach
like a focused wind
out of the North;
the explosive abrasion
up the slope

to a full-stop;
the blaze that gorged
itself finally to a flicker;
and the sooty trail
of what remained

quiet now except
for the items
(those mute appurtenances)
that began to chatter
as never before:

cameras flung away
in mid-exposure;
earrings isolated
from their owner
and from each other;

a flight bag that had rubbed
somebody's shoulder
since 1964; a shoe;
a cap; a wristwatch;
and a diary dedicated

to the glory of God
who had never been one
to break the quiet
who had looked away
at the wrong moment

who had been fooled too
by the blend of white
who had never actually
made it
that far South.

[1999]

Censorship   [CD 2.12]

after Karl Vennberg

Had they allowed the questions
to be voiced, we could have expected answers
where there were none
or we could have spoken the truth
where the truth could make a difference.

Had we at least had a typewriter to hand
and had they not confiscated the means of reproduction
we could have eked out our argument
and distributed it in the streets
we might have managed
a leaflet containing a few refusing words
scrawled in pencil or in blood

had they not forbidden the abuse of paper
had one of us had a pencil
or blood to spare

For had we had a typewriter
and had the truth been of any importance
we could have put our case
in a reasonable way in letters to the editor
set out in paragraphs and nicely punctuated
but because the times were neither reasonable nor nice
we could have uttered our anger
in uppercase and in exclamation marks
but because it is bad manners to shout
in this nation of the understatement
we could have taken to the streets
and marched in a silence
that would shame them into prohibiting silence

But they allowed us no questions and no typewriters
least of all any answers
paper was too precious to commit to writing
there was no more lead in our pencil
and our blood was too dilute
We had shouted ourselves hoarse and besides
we no longer had a case to put.

[2003]

Bill Sewell was born in Athens, Greece, in 1951 and spent his childhood in Southern Europe, the Middle East and England, where he received his primary-school education. He came to New Zealand at age fourteen.

Sewell was educated at the Universities of Auckland and Otago, completing a PhD in German at the latter, where he also lectured. Thereafter, he worked as an editor with John McIndoe and the University of Otago Press. In 1981 and 1982 he was awarded the Burns Fellowship at the University of Otago and in 1982 published his first volume of poetry, *Solo Flight*. His next collection, *Wheels Within Wheels*, was released in 1983. A third collection, *Making the Far Land Glow*, appeared in 1986. Sewell had three further volumes of poetry published before his death in January 2003: *Erebus* (1999), *El Sur* (2001) and *The Ballad of Fifty-one* (2003).

In the late 1980s, Sewell moved to Wellington and took a law degree at Victoria University, after which he worked as a legal researcher for the New Zealand Law Commission. From 1991 to 2002 he was co-editor of *New Zealand Books*. Sewell also co-edited a number of non-fiction works and three collections of poetry.

He was posthumously awarded the first Lauris Edmond Memorial Award for Poetry in 2003.

POETRY:
Solo Flight. Dunedin: University of Otago Press, 1982.
Wheels Within Wheels. Dunedin: University of Otago Press, 1983.
Making the Far Land Glow. Dunedin: McIndoe, 1986.
Erebus: A Poem. Christchurch: Hazard Press, 1999.
El Sur. Wellington: Pemmican Press, 2001.
The Ballad of Fifty-one. Wellington: HeadworX, 2003.

PROSE:
A Guide to the Rimutaka Forest Park, Wellington: GP Books, 1989.

EDITED:
New Zealand Books: A Quarterly Review. Wellington: Peppercorn Press, 1991–2002.
[with Jeanette Stace]. *Balancing on Blue*.Wellington: New Zealand Poetry Society, 1991.
[with Jeanette Stace]. *Ginger Stardust: A Selection of Poems and Haiku from the 1992 New Zealand International Poetry Competition*. Wellington: New Zealand Poetry Society, 1992.
Sons of the Fathers: New Zealand Men Write About Their Fathers. Auckland: Tandem Press, 1997.
[with Lauris Edmond and Harry Ricketts]. *Under Review: A Selection from* New Zealand Books *1991–1996*. Lincoln: Lincoln University Press, 1997.
[with Lauris Edmond]. *Essential New Zealand Poems*. Auckland: Godwit, 2001.

DAVID EGGLETON (B. 1952)

[CD 2.13] **Poem for the Unknown Tourist**

Greetings!
No stranger land than New Zespri
welcomes you all –
living anachronism,
Victorian antique,
antipodean geyserland,
inflamed appendix,
coathangers bent to shape outlines,
towers of five-cent tuatara reaching to hard-won paradise.

Land pronounced Soup Pea Ham,
land of omnipresent darkness,
land of pods of Family Fun Runners,
land where mutton falls tied to a golden parachute,
falling falling falling,
land where the name Massey hangs on the air like gunsmoke.

As unleaded islands make backcountry overtures,
our hills reverberate to the sound of gallows
being built for the end of the golden wether;
reverberate to memorial ovations
for the Lovelock lap of honour;
reverberate to whitebait in the surf
going ballistic at the umpteenth Hadlee hat-trick.

Take our camping grounds as you find them,
the pastoral exposition renovated as novelty toy,
cowsheds cut out of corrugated tin,
corkscrewing slides and water cannon,
paintball war games and lasertronics.
Flock to follow our flocks;
be shutterbugs clustering at scenic windows;

our creeks leak from reservoirs of dammed emotion;
our dreams are landfill in a well-known ocean.

Let an orienteering team
of giggling geisha girls ride tandem mountain bikes
through Cathedral Square;
let foreign language, do-wop, a capella choirs be heard
in shopping centres;
let wide-bodied new arrivals
try new fast automatic toilets,
and knock back noble rot in vineyard after vineyard,
and milk the odd sacred cow,
and be presented with kiwifruit the size of a baby.

May the bungee-jumper yodel breakfast
over the Remarkables;
may the smack of willow on leathered rump
be to your liking;
may our motels be rusted to perfection;
may you not be dismayed when everything within reason
is out of season.

As the old Pacific hand, tattooed and weatherbeaten,
rows you ashore,
as the pre-dawn hush is broken by chainsaw roar,
as you hold yourself back from the zeal of the land,
may we remain evergreen, ever thine, Aotearoa.

[2001]

Teen Angel [CD 2.14]

Behind stone shades of hard black glass,
Death the Teen Angel comes looming up fast

Boo, it's Drivetime down the Great White Way,
batting past suburbs, and Around the Bays.

Got his shotaway smile, got a double-barrelled jaw,
got a souped-up hearse – a flaming ex-police car.

Drunk-driving Death's Head, thousand metre stare;
from car wreck to car wreck his career careers.

Teen angel boy racer teen angel boy racer.

Branded, shakes a smoke loose from the packet;
to ease his graveyard itch wants to kick the bucket.

Wheelie-spin take-off, then floor it and swerve,
casket snakes writhing from beyond the grave.

Going at a hundred clicks against the clock;
curve sweeping sixty seconds, racing to a stop.

His passengers, we ride the rattle of Death Row,
to vanishing points, to a collection of black holes.

To vanishing points, to a collection of black holes.
Teen angel boy racer teen angel boy racer.

[2001]

David Eggleton began reciting his poetry in the New Zealand rock music scene of the early 1980s and he has since toured on the cabaret circuit in Australia, the United States, Europe and Britain, where he won the London *Time Out* Street Entertainer of the Year Award for Poetry. These days he regularly performs his poetry in schools, universities, pubs, clubs and cafes all over New Zealand.

His first poetry collection, *South Pacific Sunrise*, was co-winner of the PEN Best First Book of Poetry Award in 1987.

A 1996 video, *For Arts Sake – Art and Politics – Performance Poet David Eggleton*, won first prize for a TV arts documentary in the Qantas Media Awards 1997. He has also collaborated with Thai filmmaker Ranitar Charitkul on the making of two award-winning short films of his poetry: *Teleprompter* (2001) and *The Cloud Forest* (2002).

He writes freelance arts criticism for magazines and newspapers (including *Art New Zealand*, *Architecture New Zealand* and *Urbis*), and has written a number of art catalogue essays. He has won the Reviewer of the Year Award four times for his book reviews.

Eggleton has collaborated with photographer Craig Potton in the production of two New Zealand scenic books: an anthology of landscape writing, *Here on Earth* (1999) (a finalist in the Montana Book Awards), and a sequence of essays entitled *Seasons: The New Zealand Year* (2001). His history of New Zealand pop music, *Ready to Fly*, was a finalist in the 2004 Montana New Zealand Book Awards.

POETRY:
Three Poems. Drawings by the author. Dunedin: Bard One, 1978.
Three Verse Epistles. Drawings by the author. Dunedin: Bard Press, 1979.
Spirit of 79. Drawings by the author. Dunedin: Bard Press, 1979.
Dole Bait. Drawings by the author. Grey Lynn, Auckland: Lancaster Publishing, 1982.
The Mad Kiwi Ranter: New Comic & Political Poems. Auckland: X-press it, 1983.
South Pacific Sunrise. Drawings by Barry Linton. Auckland: Penguin, 1986.
People of the Land. Drawings by Lesley Maclean. Auckland: Penguin, 1988.
Poetry Demon [sound and music CD]. Wellington: Jayrem Records, 1993.
Empty Orchestra. Auckland: Auckland University Press, 1995.
RhymingPlanet. Wellington: Steele Roberts, 2001.
Versifier [sound and music CD]. Dunedin: Yellow Eye Records, 2002.
Fast Talker. Auckland: Auckland University Press, 2006.

PROSE:
After Tokyo (short fiction, with drawing by Robin Conway). Auckland: Earl of Seacliff Art Workshop, 1987.
Seasons: The New Zealand Year / Nga Wa o te Tau. Photographs by Craig Potton. Nelson: Craig Potton Publishing, 2001.
Ready to Fly: The Story of New Zealand Pop Music. Nelson: Craig Potton Publishing, 2003.
Into the Light: A History of New Zealand Photography. Illustrated. Nelson: Craig Potton Publishing, 2006.

EDITED:
Tango, 'a literary rage': Auckland University Literary Handbook 1982. Auckland: Auckland University Students' Association, 1982.
Here on Earth: The Landscape in New Zealand Literature. Photographs by Craig Potton. Nelson: Craig Potton Publishing, 1999.

GRAHAM LINDSAY (B. 1952)

[CD 2.15] **Playground**

The sun's hot on the playground
the bell has rung and what have we learned?

Maybe this one thing, maybe some other
pebble-weights in our brain!

Only a few things are for sure
mostly to do with time.

So we got out of that classroom at the end of primary school
and we got out of that classroom at the end of high school

and where are we?
Epochs have passed

the spring of morning, autumn of afternoon
midday's shadowless mysteries

on the fencerail overlooking the playground
two five-year-olds rolling down a bank kissing

Flagstaff sinking in mist and dusk
we are here and we don't know how.

[1986]

Cloud silence

[CD 2.16]

There has always been
someone

seated
under this tree, looking up

the harbour valley
over rush-studded
paddocks glistening

after rain.
And I'm the first

        you want to say
you saw the hills

        that seemed like home
ladders of sunlight leaned
against clouds, then the clouds marched
seaward like ranks of ghost soldiers.
The point is

to stop writing. Stop
using language to protect
yourself from the full

implications of the world – the world says
Look at me, I dare you to
I dare you to see.
        You tilt your head

back and look up
at the tree.
A ray peers

into the room
of your eye . . .

*

Why is our art so introverted?
It doesn't mean a thing

to the seagull or sun
the clouds don't understand
a word

their language is silence
and movement and colour.

Here on the face of it – there
behind a mask. This far
above ground

                    in 360° cinemas
as the present rolls

[1994]

[CD 2.17] **Life in the Queen's English**

Images of the grass lift

off the grass kinds of green
I've seen before and I know

if I get down on hands and knees
I'll not necessarily improve

my understanding of the feel
of grass. Watching shapes

in the rock garden alter
with walking past, a plane

of grey gravel tips . . . Lovers
learning to walk together exit

from the park awkwardly.
Pines like green clouds

a pantheon of Lombardy
poplars. The way words

like images lift
pull back peel

from their referents, leave us

longing for the intimacy
that preceded their birth

[1994]

Chink   [CD 2.18]

When you announced from the backdoor
it was dinnertime, I was in translation,
holed up in the no man's land, a coffin's length wide,
between the garage and the fence,
drinking the kind of drink that improves
with a glass or two and (more to the point,
being a 'non-smoker') smoking a rollie.
My other ear was getting an earbashing
from the milkman's inane jingle *Greensleeves*
which was holding to ransom the whole suburb.
In the incidental silence which overlapped
like tiny estuarine waves, I was tuning in

to the song of snails, the murmur of air
like a river / river like air, the rattle of dog collar
as through the fence Marshall scratched his side;
sounds in other cultures of air.
When the clatter of choppingboard-on-bench
arrived from the kitchen, I was lost inside
the pulse inside my temple, everything erased
by the smooth undersides of the walnut tree,
the pittosporum leaves, which only recently
had found a place in my heart – *There's always*
been a place in our heart for you, they chorused
in a soundless whisper that seemed to echo
from the origin of the universe, lifting their skirts,
so to speak, and cha-cha-cha-ing sideways,
just as there's always been a place in yours for us.
Where the sun's grace fell through a chink
in the palings, the retinas of rainwater on young
honeysuckle leaves and I eyed each other.
The next moment, not surprisingly, was altogether
different from the one that had gone before
and which had promised so much, confronting me
with obsolete folding doors, surplus spouting,
tannalised offcuts, cannibalised bikes, a forsaken
homebrew barrel, the distance of neighbours.
If only I'd played my cards right, I whimpered,
and snuggled up to opportunities, rather than
shrugging them off – the story of my life, etc. etc.
Hard on the heels of which line of thought came this,
namely, that in the cold hard world of contingency
perhaps Judas is the real hero, caught as he was
between the rock and hard place of the question
whether to believe. After all, some days you can't
understand how anybody could think otherwise;
other days, how you could have thought that yourself.
Having determined to let whatever came to pass
play its hand, I glimpsed my father's face
sizing me up from the bottom of the glass.

[2003]

Graham Lindsay was born in Wellington in 1952. He was educated at the University of Canterbury (BA, 1976) and the Christchurch College of Education (Diploma of Teaching, 1989). He has since worked in a variety of short-term or part-time jobs including driving, library work and teaching. He has two sons and one grandson and lives in England.

His first book, *Thousand-Eyed Eel*, an account of the historic Maori land march of 1975, appeared from Alan Loney's Hawk Press in 1976. Since then he has published six more collections of poems. He also edited the magazine *Morepork* from 1979 to 1980.

He has read at a number of literary festivals and his poems have appeared widely in anthologies.

POETRY:
Thousand-Eyed Eel. Taylors Mistake: Hawk Press, 1976.
Public. Dunedin: Ridge-Pole, 1980.
Big Boy. Auckland: Auckland University Press, 1986.
Return to Earth. Christchurch: Hazard Press, 1991.
The Subject. Auckland: Auckland University Press, 1994.
Legend of the Cool Secret. Christchurch: Sudden Valley Press, 1999.
Lazy Wind Poems. Auckland: Auckland University Press, 2003.

EDITED:
Morepork. 1–3. Dunedin: Ridge-Pole (1979–80).

BIOGRAPHY:
Jack Ross, 'A Conversation with Graham Lindsay'. In *Complete with Instructions*. Ed. David Howard. Christchurch: Firebrand, 2001.

IAIN SHARP (B. 1953)

[CD 2.19] **Amnesty Day**

Woke this morning at 5am, cursing my sluggishness,
cursing the cold, the dark, the rain, cursing the long crawl
rain would bring to the motorway, cursing my maniac
promise to plonk a review of an untouched novel
on the deputy editor's desk by 9am, cursing
the novel line by line as I scrambled through it,
cursing myself for having no opinion of the novel,
cursing the novelist, cursing Denzel bloody Washington
whose Oscar-winning performance I watched last night
instead of touching the untouched novel.

Denzel's normally so noble. This is his big breakout;
he plays such a prick I cheered at the end when half
a dozen hard-faced Russians jumped out of snazzy
black cars and blew him into beef stroganoff with Uzi
machine guns. His death takes a full minute of screen time.
The Israel Military Industry Limited website says
the ever dependable Uzi, which continues to sell well,
fires 600 rounds a minute. Even allowing for the fact
some Russian gangsters can't shoot for shit, I figure
Denzel gets shot at least 3000 times.

That statistic's on my mind instead of my review
(of which I have no opinion), as I join the long crawl
to the newspaper's arse entrance in Minnie Street. That's
Minnie as in Minnie Mouse, but it's a small street too
and a truck the size of a train consumes all of it,
forcing me to trudge to the office in the rain,
cursing, afraid by the time I move to my main Thursday job
in the city library's hidden recesses I'll miss
out on the early bird parking at the Civic Car Park.
Prices come 9.30 triple. I arrive at 9.25

and, hell, the early birds have gone to the worms.
It's more like a conference of fowls. Crowds gawk
at the ticket machine, confused by its demands, wanting
receipts. As prices triple, I come to hate them all,
imagine an Uzi in each mitt, another triggered
by my toes. I'm shooting each of them 3000 times,
really getting into it, loathing and slaying everybody –
truck drivers, car drivers, deputy editors, novelists,
early birds, Minnie Mouse. Then suddenly I remember
Hell, it's Amnesty Day! I'm meant to read at Riemke's shindig.

Amnesty: from the Latin amnestia – forgetting,
same root as amnesia,
a selective amnesia, if you please.
For mercy's sake, folks, forget everything you've heard.

[2004]

Two Minute Poem [CD 2.20]

It's long enough to drown, pray,
propose marriage, begin divorce
proceedings, boil an egg,
have an orgasm, have an aneurysm,
convert to Islam.

Bob Hawke in his prime could down
three gallons of ale in two minutes.
Barbara Cartland in her dotage could
declaim nine pages of dripping romance.
Across Nevada's Black Rock Desert
one October in a car named Thrust
fighter pilot Andy Green drove
42 kilometres in two minutes. Shoooosh,
that's halfway from here to Huntly.

In two minutes Ian Thorpe can swim
200 metres on his back. A Concord
can fly from here to Huntly five times.
Messalina once made love to six
strapping gladiators in two minutes.
None was quite as she imagined.
Every minute Bill Gates' wealth expands
by $610,000, just imagine.

Minutes were invented in 1656
by Dutch boffin Christiaan Huygens
(Descartes' precision-mad protégé).
Before that, nobody gave a fuck.
Kupe sailed by the stars across
the shark-filled, heaving Pacific
never knowing what a minute was,
never missing a beat.

A minute of course is 60 seconds
and a second officially is
nine billion
192 million
631 thousand
and 770 periods of
the radiation corresponding to
the transition between the two
hyperfine levels of cesium-133.

As far as I'm aware
I've never seen even
a coarse level of cesium-133.
It moves too fast for me.
I live from minute to minute.

[2004]

Iain Sharp is an Auckland-based journalist, poet, reviewer, newspaper and magazine columnist and librarian. Born in Scotland in 1953, he was educated at the University of Auckland, where he completed a PhD in English in 1982. He has published four solo collections of verse and has had his poetry and short fiction featured in, among other places, *Landfall*, *Islands*, *Printout*, *Sport* and *Poetry New Zealand*. His book reviews, criticism and interviews appear regularly in the *Sunday Star-Times*.

POETRY:
Why Mammals Shiver. Auckland: One Eyed Press, 1981.
She's Trying to Kidnap the Blind Person. Auckland: Hard Echo Press, 1985.
The Pierrot Variations. Auckland: Hard Echo Press, 1985.
[with Suzanne Chapman]. *Two Poets*. Auckland: Auckland English Association, 1985.
The Singing Harp, Paekakariki: Earl of Seacliff Art Workshop, 2004.

PROSE:
Sail the Spirit. Auckland: Reed, 1994.

JANET CHARMAN (B. 1954)

[CD 2.21] **'they say that in paradise'**

they say
that in paradise

the souls
of the martyrs

are met
by dozens

of willing
virgins

but women
are matter

and so
don't ascend there

leave us
in dust?

that is
outrageous

no
it's just

what
happens

to men's souls
too

but
they

don't admit
it

[2002]

ready steady [CD 2.22]

in the bucket
my hand gropes
for a peg

the grass knot
i start at
is not a *weta*
it is not

remembering
the fatty podge
of a loved baby

realising
others have walked
alone through this house
at night

others
have been the only one
stirring
in the milk soup
of the moonlight

trying not to use
words which will decay

not *telephone*
say 'make a call'
not *cd*
say 'music playing'

calling and playing music
someone singing

burying them

[2002]

[CD 2.23] *from* **wake up to yourself**

for Mary Barnard, translator of Sappho

going to work

darkness
dispersing

the sky
fills

with
light

rain
falls

the heavy weight
of a hollow boat

leaves
my heart

[2007]

but she wanted one

he gift wrapped
an ironing board
for her birthday

another time
she was mashing the egg
for the sandwiches
and sousing
the thermos
when he vetoed the picnic

'I don't go working every blessed morning
to spend my weekends on Paekakariki beach'

still she threw the food in the baskets
and told us to find our coats
we were going to go
as a family
and enjoy ourselves

crowding in the train
we watch them closely
bent double
by the wind on the over-pass we
forget to stinging sand on the shore
sheets us freezing to the
bus shelter

where he dropped the milk
smash
at our feet

[2002]

cuckoo in the nest

the pigeon fancier
sent us home
from the paddock
with egg gifts
for our Mother

who has long hair
and fur
under her arms

'oh he likes me' she says
poaching the pale yolks
'it annoys your Father'

i'm sent around to the glasshouses
with Half a Crown for
The Catholic Couple

wait for the change

'Wasn't there some?'

they gave me a brown bag of bursting red
green tufted fruit
i won't eat

down the dark hall
half asleep
some trouble or other

in the hot kitchen
she's leaning over
his eye
with a dropper

when they see   me
up after eleven
this is
surprise
they're feeling
bustled back to bed

just as if
there's a life they lived
before i did

[2002]

injection [CD 2.26]

up the narrow stair
to where the needle
and the glass syringe
swim in the sterilising medium

the smiling Sister
with her hair-gripped veil
leans over

who's going first?
not me i will
and the sleeve
rolled up

the wetted swab
hurried on

the soft gauge of
myself
under her hand
then stinging going in
and in and on

the bead of blood
the stamp drawn
downstairs across the street to Adams Bruce
Confectionery

where chocolate fish float
belly up

and in my arm
the throb
the insult

[2002]

Janet Charman grew up in the Hutt Valley and Taranaki. She did a nursing apprenticeship as a teenager, and has had aiding jobs in psychiatry and social work. She has also been a radio copywriter, a telephone operator, a bar woman and, after completing an MA in English literature, a tutor at the University of Auckland. She was their writer in residence in 1997. She is now a secondary-school teacher and lives in Avondale with her family.

Sexual politics is a persistent theme in all her poetry. Most recently, in *cold snack*, AUP (2007), she takes a hard look at the mysteries of teaching, the joy of television and the unavoidability of time travel.

POETRY:
2 Deaths in 1 Night: Poems. Auckland: New Women's Press, 1985.
Red Letter. Auckland: Auckland University Press, 1992.
End of the Dry. Auckland: Auckland University Press, 1995.
Rapunzel, Rapunzel. Auckland: Auckland University Press, 1999.
Snowing Down South. Auckland: Auckland University Press, 2002.
Cold Snack. Auckland: Auckland University Press, 2007.

PAULA GREEN (B. 1955)

greek salad

[CD 2.27]

for me
she washes
lettuce
plump black olives
I so scarcely
fed her

[1997]

oven baked salmon

[CD 2.28]

I like my fat cooking pot
I like my fat wild heart

[1997]

afternoon tea with Virginia Woolf

[CD 2.29]

over the flower beds
over the fumes and steams
over the neck of a horse
over the same broad leaves
over the limb
over the pastry and fruit
over the mass and edge
over the shell against a stone
over the one bright feather
over the sharp wedges

over the pressure of the morning
over the swift scales
over the glaze of china
over the bulk of a cupboard

[1997]

[CD 2.30]   **Two Minutes Westward**

We take ourselves like mountain goats up the muddy
track, cloud before rock, rock before flax because
in the stillness we find the noise of an ocean
sinking roots sunk fierce
into how to be westward.
Westcoast skin. Westcoast blood. Westcoast bone.
Stepping into this sweet cyclone of silence
we are pinned to the inlet cool and spare
like a roving eye
disappearing and feeding on heavenly wings
halfway to paradise
with a divine map for romance
those perspiring sonnets and me doubled back
laughing like death.
This is high and on the edge
vertigo looping the Te Henga cliff tops
behind us a flower might blossom
a musical note might flare
but one thing's for sure
here on cold mornings
here where love is snacking
the risk of heights punctuates
a risk we take
our heartbeats startled at the startled kereru.
A word for his skin
a word for his bone
a word for his blood

then memory steadies the erring waterfall
the white plume of the heron all dried up.
Still I keep the ancient preserve of kauri
stuck in my guts
some kind of brace
because I will hurl
all the old figures over the edge
in one foul swoop
down there into the seething
steaming black sanded
heart of the west coast sea.
Holding his hand at midnight
beneath the starry sky
I will try and let Ulysses loose
and Virgil's honey tongued
camminiamo a ritornare
nel chiaro mondo?
Vediamo le cose belle
che porta il cielo?
Holding his hand at midnight and kissing those
amber lips here in the light belief
that a word will dig the pit
for the featherweight myth.
Turn your head my dearest to the left
stand still and hear the droning brook
or the otherwhere hum of the bee.
Still. Stand still. Turn your ear to the right
and hear the wind rubbing across the track
a pocket of nectar and linseed oil
pressing against my spine.
Would we take a boat home
across the wild comfort?

[2004]

Paula Green lives in Auckland with painter Michael Hight and their two children. She completed her doctoral thesis on Italian women's literature of the twentieth century in 2004. She has taught in the Italian, film and television studies and women's studies departments at the University of Auckland.

Auckland University Press has published all of her collections of poetry to date, *Cookhouse* (1997), *Chrome* (2000), *Crosswind* (2004) and, most recently, *Flamingo Bendalingo* (2006). Her essays, poetry and short fiction have appeared in journals in New Zealand, Australia, Canada, the United States, Great Britain and India. She has appeared at the Auckland Writers & Readers Festival, Seeing Voices and participated in New Zealand Book Council reading tours.

Green founded a series of poetry readings 'The Alba Readings' in the early 1990s. She was also programme co-ordinator for the Seeing Voices poetry festival.

POETRY:

Cookhouse. Drawings by Michael Hight. Auckland: Auckland University Press, 1997.

Chrome. Auckland: Auckland University Press, 2000.

Crosswind. Auckland: Auckland University Press, 2004.

[with 50 children]. *Flamingo Bendalingo: Poems from the Zoo*. Illustrated by Michael Hight. Auckland: Auckland University Press, 2006.

Making Lists for Frances Hodgkins. Auckland: Auckland University Press, forthcoming.

VIVIENNE PLUMB (B. 1955)

A Letter from my Daughter

[CD 2.31]

The trees are tall here, and everything
grows fast in the hot sun and heavy
rain. The wet has come, and butterflies
are the size of small birds. There are ticks
and leeches, enormous mosquitoes,
spiders, flies, thick striped snakes and green
ants, and they all bite. The rainforest
can be dark at night. And these mountains
are as green as their ferny gullies.
Sometimes the clouds engulf a whole huge
mountain top. The beaches have marvellous
shells and the sand lies silky and pure
white. You can pick coconuts, you can
pick as many as you like, and then
hollow out the smooth brown husks to use
for bowls. I have seen parrots, fruit bats,
black water snakes and tree rats. Mangoes,
bananas and pawpaws are growing
wild. During the wet, the sky becomes
deep violet and then next minute
the rain arrives in sheets. Water floods
the bridges and roads, and we cannot
reach Cairns. Because of the rain, local
houses are built on stilts, but below
the ridge down in the Commune we live
in old cars, in yellow bamboo huts,
or in treehouses under plastic.
I often walk along the railway
tracks and over the railway bridges.
There are big lemon trees by the tracks
further up (good for tropical
ulcers). I do not like the cane toads.

And now finally I must finish
this letter, but know that my spirit
astral travels at night, and therefore
I am nearer you more than ever
before. Always OM, your daughter Jane,
who has now been renamed Yasmeen
Shima Mogra Ashanti Cloud Burst.

[2004]

[CD 2.32] **The Vegan Bar and Gaming Lounge**

I hate places with names
like *Cafe Bleu*.
I thought I saw a
Vegan Bar and Gaming Lounge,
my mistake, it was *Vegas*.
Clubs with names like *Hot Chilli*
are trying to tell us
that we will have a good time.
The birds were singing
as I crossed the dusky bridge,
in the park the damp leaves
were as big as my hands,
they had fallen into corpse
shaped piles, the carriage
lamps were lit.

I hate places with names
like *The Olde Taverne*,
or *Aunty Val-Mae's Country Kitchen*,
there's generally a hair
in the scones, or the drink
is poured with little generosity.
When I rose to depart
there were leaves like hands

all around me.
In the hotel I woke in the
obsequious dark, not knowing
where I am, where I was,
not knowing.

[2004]

The Tank

[CD 2.33]

for Victor

I hum and write, I hum under
my breath and keep writing.
A good bit about the goldfish
in the tank at Bats. The tank
sits on one of the Bats booth
tables. There are three fish.
Two look like ordinary gold
fish, but the third has really
black rings on its eyes, like
it's been bashed by the others.
And Victor remarks: *Heidi says*
if you tap the tank like this,
you could give them a heart
attack. And he taps the tank.
And I guess that's what it is
we can feel sometimes,
it's Victor's big fat finger
tapping the tank.

[2000]

Vivienne Plumb has a BA in English literature and art history from Victoria University, Wellington, and completed her MA there in 2000. She began writing after attending Bill Manhire's creative writing course at Victoria University. Her short fiction collection, *The Wife Who Spoke Japanese in her Sleep*, was published by University of Otago Press and was awarded the 1994 Hubert Church Prose Award (Best First Book Award).

Her first playscript, *Love Knots*, was awarded the 1993 Bruce Mason Playwrighting Award. It premiered at Circa Theatre and was published in 1994. Her first collection of poetry, *Salamanca*, was published in 1998 by HeadworX and her second, *Avalanche*, was published by Pemmican Press in June 2000.

During 2000 she was invited to perform her 'live-art lecture', *Fact or Fiction: Meditations on Mary Finger*, at the 5th International Women Playwrights Conference in Athens, Greece.

In 2001 Plumb held the 2001 Buddle Findlay Sargeson Fellowship which she used to complete her first novel, *Secret City*, published in 2003 by Cape Catley Press (Auckland).

She was writer in residence at Massey University in 2006 and her play *The Cape* will premiere at Circa Theatre in 2007.

POETRY:
Salamanca. Wellington: HeadworX, 1998.
Avalanche. Wellington: Pemmican Press, 2000.
Nefarious. Wellington: HeadworX, 2004.
Scarab: A Poetic Documentary. Wellington: Seraph Press, 2005.
Doppelgänger. Wellington: Earl of Seacliff Art Workshop, 2006.

PLAYS:
Love Knots. Wellington: Women's Play Press, 1994.

PROSE:
The Wife Who Spoke Japanese in her Sleep. Dunedin: University of Otago Press, 1993.
The Diary as a Positive in Female Adult Behaviour. Wellington: HeadworX, 1999.
Secret City. Auckland: Cape Catley, 2003.

EDITED:
Between these Hills. Wellington: 1991.
Sevensome. Wellington: Calliope Press, 1993.
Red Light Means Stop: Six Super Solos from Aotearoa New Zealand. Wellington: The Women's Play Press, 2003.

APIRANA TAYLOR (B. 1955)

Sad Joke on a Marae

[CD 2.34]

Tihei Mauriora I called
Kupe Paikea Te Kooti
Rewi and Te Rauparaha
I saw them
grim death and wooden ghosts
carved on the meeting house wall.

In the only Maori I knew I called
Tihei Mauriora
Above me the tekoteko raged.
He ripped his tongue from his mouth
and threw it at my feet.

Then I spoke.
My name is Tu the freezing worker
Ngati D.B. is my tribe.
The pub is my Marae.
My fist is my taiaha.
Jail is my home.

Tihei Mauriora I cried.
They understood
the tekoteko and the ghosts
though I said nothing but
Tihei Mauriora
for that's all I knew

[1979]

Parihaka

We never knew
about Parihaka
it was never
taught anywhere
except maybe
around the fires
of Parihaka
itself at night
when stories
are told
of the soldiers
who came
with guns
to haul us up
by the roots
like trees
from our land
though the Prophets
called peace peace
it was never
taught at school
it was all hushed up
how we listened
to the Prophets
Tohu, Te Whiti
who called
Peace Rire rire
Paimarire
but the only
peace the soldiers knew
spoke through
the barrels
of their guns
threatening
our women, children
it was never

taught or spoken
how we
were shackled
led away to the caves
and imprisoned
for ploughing our land.

[2001]

Hinemoa's daughter

[CD 2.36]

her hair is so long
you could plait it all the way to the moon
and weave it with a sprinkling of stars

she writes poetry
as only the muse can write

when she smiles
she melts the heart of God

'I'm from Te Arawa' she says

she shows me her litany of scars
they climb like ladders
up the insides of her wrists

deep savage cuts to the bone
speak of her youth and the countless times
she sent herself along the path of the spirits
and sought the solace of Hine nui te po

like her tipuna Hinemoa
she swam the lake
but her lake was of fire and death
broken bottles drunken fights
smashed families shattered and scattered whanau

and she made it
she crossed the troubled water
and found her tane who loves her
more deeply than the heart can tell

in the city of the lost
they raise many fine young children
with aroha

[2002]

six million

'Oh Api'

my friend Wolfgang weeps
as we walk up the road to Dachau
'you are proud of your ancestors
how can I be proud of mine
my father was a Nazi
we fought over the dinner table
we've not spoken for twenty years'

tears flood from Wolfgang's eyes

'i've never been able to visit the camp
i've lived here all my life'

brother Wolfgang weeps

his karanga to the dead rises
into the dull grey sky

the spirits listen in silence

as we walk up the road
on the corpses of six million dead Jews

[2002]

Apirana Taylor was born in Wellington in 1955, of Te Whanau a Apanui, Ngati Porou and Ngati Ruanui descent. In addition to poetry, he has written short stories, criticism and a novel, *He Tangi Aroha* (1993). Taylor is also an actor and playwright and was a prominent member of the Maori theatre cooperative Te Ohu Whakaari. He has taught drama and creative writing at Whitireia Community Polytechnic and has held writing fellowships at Massey University (1996) and the University of Canterbury (2002).

POETRY:

Eyes of the Ruru. Wellington: Voice Press, 1979.
[with Lindsay Rabbitt and L. E. Scott]. *3 Shades*. Wellington: Voice Press, 1981.
Soft Leaf Falls of the Moon. Auckland: Pohutukawa Press, 1996.
Te Ata Kura / The Red Tipped Dawn. Christchurch: Canterbury University Press, 2004.

PROSE:

He Rau Aroha. Auckland: Penguin, 1986.
Ki Te Ao: New Stories. Auckland: Penguin, 1990.
He Tangi Aroha. Wellington: Huia Publishers, 1993.
Bell Bird is Small: Short Stories. Auckland: Pohutukawa Press, 2000.

PLAYS:

Kohanga and Whāea Kairau. Auckland: Pohutukawa Press, 1999.

ANNE FRENCH (B. 1956)

[CD 2.38] **The new museology**

a found poem

They don't read, of course.
We know that. The best
international research
tells us so. They
hardly read their Lotto
tickets, so why
should they read
labels? ('Even yours, Anne.')
The magic of the real object
is an anti-climax.
Face it. They care only about
experiences. We know;
our research says
their recall of the sponsor's
name is 67 per cent *unprompted*.
Our hi-energy attractions are
competing with other leisure
activities in the whole region
– Disneyland, even.
So what's the take-out,
what's at the top of the brand
pyramid?

Bungy-jumping
from the Clyde High Dam
of culture
but no vaka, thanks,
we're customer-
focused. And no art,
either. Babies in flowerpots

have greater unprompted
recognition than those
smears of oil
that necessary protection.

Which leaves us
with this.
It's a dark ride, it's I-Max, it's 3-D
on a 360° screen,
with maximum wow
factor, it's terror tourism
with or without a camera
mounted
on the front forks

it's the world, folks,
uninterpreted
and full of natural language
it's yours to be in, yours to
misunderstand in your own way
so take your treasure
paddle off in it
hang it in some sordid
back street of taste
or bury it, go on, bury it
in a swamp
till we recover our senses

[1998]

Trout

for Harold Marshall

At six o'clock on a cool Southland evening
we go stalking. Just like old times –
one light rod, all your special gear, a certain
knowledge of fishy behaviour. They rise

and rise, mouthing at the water's thick
surface, biding their time in the pool below the riffle,
feeding on whatever hatches over a slow river
around six pm in a Southland summer –

but not your nymph, perfectly placed, drifting
to them down the current. This is how I first learned
the habits of fish, watching you. We sneaked up
on snapper at Bradshaw Cove, cast flies to kahawai,

trolled kingy lures, netted piper. How I learned
many other things, not well: boat handling,
crew handling, the weather, the Gulf, sailing
at night, being the skipper. All the words

to 'The Road to Mandalay'. Up on the bank,
tucked out of sight behind my willow, I can see
they're not eating what you're offering.
I head back to the warm house and the cricket.

One lesson learned. 'You'll have to stop
calling me "Skip",' you say next morning.
It's hot and still. I think about the trout,
hanging like shadows in the brown pool.

[2004]

Acute

[CD 2.40]

for Kevin Dew

He knows exactly where to place his hand.
It's cool, like an instrument. Beneath
its dry touch, the pain burns – here,

inside the left sacrum; and here, and here.
He numbers the joints of my body
as a lover might, and says their names,

remembering them, their histories.
He imagines the curves of my spine,
its flexion points, where the curve changes,

where the mechanical load intensifies,
where it passes in front of or behind
gravity's line of force. I'm pinned

in his imagination to the Earth,
one G hauling on this cage of bone
pulling it down to humus and decay.

He is gentle. Respectful of the pain,
he wonders if I can turn over.
Offers me his arm. Finds it again

in clavicle and scapula. It blooms,
red embers in grey ash. Muscles knot
around it, like hands cupped round

something precious. He is tender,
patiently stretches out the knots of pain,
appraises my state of balance, releases me.

[2004]

Uncle Ron's last surprise

New Year's Eve 1993, and Uncle Ron
has us all fooled. I'm walking the Milford
Track, and he's flat on his back in Cook

Hospital, dying. By the time I've got to a phone-
box in Te Anau, Auntie Jean's pranged the car
on the worst corner to Tiniroto ('Ron will kill me

when he finds out') and he's sitting up in bed
looking much better and cheeking the nurses.
For a few days there Uncle Ron and the panel-

beater are going neck and neck. This time
it's for good, the Grim Reaper being that much
more efficient second time around.

The family converges on Neilson St and the kitchen's
steamy with catching up on thirty years. Tony's home
from Scotland, married, the tallest cousin, no longer

a tow-haired barefoot kid scrapping with Peter
in the dirt; and Jennifer drives through the Gorge
in her Renault 5 at night. We're all just like ourselves

only more so; except for Uncle Ron,
who's pretending to be a small pale man
in his second-best suit in a coffin in the spare room.

[2004]

Anne French was born in Wellington in 1956. She was educated at Wellington Girls'
College and Victoria University, where she received an MA in English Literature in 1980.
    She worked in publishing for twenty years, mainly for Oxford University Press
New Zealand (where she was the New Zealand publisher). Subsequently she established
Te Papa Press, and was publisher at Te Papa for more than five years. In 2002 she left

publishing to work in science funding, and is now international relationships manager at the Foundation for Research, Science, and Technology.

Anne French's first book, *All Cretans Are Liars*, won the New Zealand Book Award for Poetry in 1988 (and also received the PEN Award for Best First Book of Poetry). Her fifth collection, *Boys' Night Out* (1998), was a finalist in the 1999 Montana New Zealand Book Awards. She was the inaugural writer in residence at Massey University in 1993.

Her interests include music, painting, and sailing. She sings in Cantoris, a Wellington chamber choir, manages Wellington Youth Sinfonietta, a youth orchestra, and her song cycle, *Wild*, set to music by Wellington composer Michael Vinten, has recently received its first performance. She is currently working on an English translation of *Love's Silence*, a collection of poems by the early twentieth-century Korean poet Han Yong-Un.

POETRY:
All Cretans are Liars. Auckland: Auckland University Press, 1987.
The Male as Evader. Auckland: Auckland University Press, 1988.
Cabin Fever. Auckland: Auckland University Press, 1990.
Seven Days on Mykonos. Auckland: Auckland University Press, 1993.
Boys' Night Out. Auckland: Auckland University Press, 1998.
Wild. Auckland: Auckland University Press, 2004.

MICHELE LEGGOTT (B. 1956)

[CD 2.42] **cairo vessel**

I

Girl
night and day, you are the One
        I lie awake till dawn   dreaming
only you beneath the moon
        and under the sun
you make my heart into a drumbeat
        stretched over the morning sky
I hear your voice and I'm gone
        all-of-me and forever   fastpost
I know how to pick you up
        if you'll just let me kneel down
nobody else in my heart but you
        nobody in yours
        but me!

I want you
        like fat and honey
you are fine linen on the bodies of the grandees
        white raiment on the bodies of the gods
you're incense at the nostril of Always
        oils from the lip of As If
you are the finger putting on my seal-ring
        and he who turns it at will
you are mandrakes in the hand of God
        a date-cake dipped in honey
        lilies set by bread
love comes tripping up and down the river
        all the days of our lives
love is a steamboat ticket
        to anywhere you want to go

we'll be together
        day in day out, I'll give you kisses
if we have to be old
        let's laugh like candied hippos
        up to our ears in mud

my god my lotus
        my blue water lily
riding with the north wind
        across the Lake of Myrrh
gentle your fingers in my hair
        your sweet breath behind my ear
blossoms float past us
        we're part of a galaxy that whirls
I want to put on sheer linen
        and go down to the river to bathe
walking a little ahead   knowing
        you're picking up the vapour trail
I'm your spice girl   I make everything
        all right

come on   follow me
        to the pool with its fringe of reeds
I'll go down into the water with you
        I'll come out with a red carp
        wriggling on my fingers for you
here it is my warrior of the beautiful weapons
        look at it and look at me
looking at you   we should kiss

Boy
little sister you're on the far bank
        and the river swirls between us
it's pulling me into the floodwaters
        and a crocodile grins on the sandbank
I wade right into the torrent
        I'm thinking about you so close so far
the crocodile's just a handbag

I zip him up and walk on those waters
      like a miracle man
your hot love makes this possible
      your water-spell is irresistible
I see the darling of my heart
      waiting faraway so close
      I can't take my eyes off you

now we're together my heart bangs
      I open my arms and you walk right in
my heart is happy   can't you feel it jump
      like a fish in a lotus pool?
the night goes on and on
      since you came to save me sweetheart

when I get you close your beautiful arms
      go around me like a princess fresh
      from Punt
you're all Missy-plant and fragrant pomades
      bundled up just for me

I kiss your lips open
      drunk on your intoxicating mouth
tell me you're having a good time
      goddess   tell me the drug works
in your heart-depths too
      as we think about a room for the night
I asked the temple girls for advice
      they said If she's your queen
      set fine linen around her body
      lay on scented white sheets
      and a whole forest of moth-orchids
you are my queen and your limbs are sails
      that take us to This
      drenched in the oils of love

2

Boy
I wish I were her pizza boy
        always on the end of a string
hey I'd bring mandrakes and lilies
        hand-delivered to her room in a jar
she'd sniff them dreamily
        and offer me all the delights of her body

I wish I were washing out her clothes
        even for just one minute
I'd be so happy just to handle
        filmy linen that had touched her body
I'd wash out the musky sweetness
        that clings to her underthings
I'd wipe my body with that party dress
        she wore yesterday to the lagoon
my joy would be complete
        ecstasy would carry me away

I wish I were that cute ring
        wrapped around her little finger
I'd feel her love
        every single day
I'd be close enough
        to steal her heart away
I wish I had all the mornings of the world
        to sit and look at her
If I could be her mirror
        this gaze would be unending
I'd be over the moon
        showing her beautiful face
to the world
        and adoring every move she makes

little sister every day I want you
        like frangipanis and the lemon tree

in blossom
the sun is high   I shake your branches
            and white stars fall on me *holà*
Mebebs flourish   Ir-trees burst into bloom
            the stone-blue flower and the mandrakes
            send out their dreamy magic
fennel runs wild   ginger festoons the paths
            hibiscus butterflies unfold everywhere
life expands
            when you're here with your spice garden
and your tropical ricochets
            let's drink birthday wine

I wish I'd been the first
            to see her blue eyes open wide
I'd do anything to keep my baby doll
            happy and here with me
why would she ever go?
            I'm the best on the block
I bring her pashtoons
            in the morning and lunations
late at night   she giggles and lets me in
            with my bread and puppet show
I'm in a spin and so is she
            that's how it works with us

I'm dizzy   we've been in bed all day
            sun swinging around us
like a camera on a trolley
            she had to run to the wharf
to catch her boat
            in a cloud of butterflies
            and off the shoulder kisses
she's banished every evil from my body
            I won't wash for a week
I want to smell of her so everyone knows
            what we've been up to
and the torment I'm going through

because I'm in public view
　　　　when I should be wrapped around her
　　　　　　world without end *amen*

I went to the beach
　　　　where her boat sailed at sundown
I'd spent the night in pain
　　　　unsure life could continue
what did I see but the sun rising
　　　　on a heart moulded in sand
white shells for butterflies
　　　　pressed into its beautiful curves

she's banished every evil from my body
　　　　I'm in orbit around her
I won't stop singing
　　　　I won't start washing
I won't [finish this line]
　　　　until we're together again

ODM 1266 + O CAIRO CGC 25218

[2005]

Michele Leggott, poet, critic and editor, was born in Stratford, Taranaki, and educated at New Plymouth Girls' High School and the University of Canterbury, graduating with an MA in English in 1979 for a thesis on the poetry of Ian Wedde. She spent 1980–85 in Canada completing a PhD on American poet Louis Zukofsky at the University of British Columbia. In 1991 she was appointed to a lectureship at the University of Auckland, where she is co-founder with Brian Flaherty of the New Zealand Electronic Poetry Centre (nzepc).

Her first book of poems, *Like This?* (1988), won the PEN Best First Book of Poetry award. *DIA* (1994) won the New Zealand Book Award for Poetry.

Much of her critical work has been concerned with the 'submerged' tradition of women poets in New Zealand. In line with this, she has edited Robin Hyde's *The Book of Nadath* (1999) and *Young Knowledge: The Poems of Robin Hyde* (2003).

POETRY:

Like This? Poems. Christchurch: Caxton Press, 1988.
Swimmers, Dancers. Auckland: Auckland University Press, 1991.
DIA. Auckland: Auckland University Press, 1994.
As Far As I Can See. Auckland: Auckland University Press, 1999.
Milk & Honey. Auckland: Auckland University Press, 2005; Cambridge: Salt, 2006.
Journey to Portugal. Auckland: Holloway Press, 2007.

PROSE:

Reading Zukofsky's 80 Flowers. Baltimore: Johns Hopkins University Press, 1989.

EDITED:

New Zealand Electronic Poetry Centre, www.nzepc.auckland.ac.nz. 2001–
Robin Hyde, *The Victory Hymn, 1935–1995*. Auckland: Holloway Press, 1995.
[with Mark Williams]. *Opening the Book: New Essays on New Zealand Writing*. Auckland: Auckland University Press, 1995.
Robin Hyde, *The Book of Nadath*. Auckland: Auckland University Press, 1999.
[with Alan Brunton and Murray Edmond]. *Big Smoke: New Zealand Poems 1960–1975*. Auckland: Auckland University Press, 2000.
Robin Hyde, *Young Knowledge: The Poems of Robin Hyde*. Auckland: Auckland University Press, 2003.

RICHARD VON STURMER (B. 1957)

Dreams [CD 2.43]

As the sun slips below the horizon, a swan closes its eyes

At a Chinese restaurant, a Chinese waiter eats his evening meal with a knife
and fork

A woman drops her child on the carpet, and instead of crying it laughs

In the car-wrecker's yard, fragments of window glass sparkle in the sunlight

A strip of red balloon hangs from the beak of a seagull

★

After a fight at school, acorns are found on the toilet floor

At the edge of a storm, someone is heard sweeping leaves

In the back garden, rain drips from the eaves of a doll's house

The sunset glows pink inside the ears of a black dog

In a takeaway bar, a machine for killing flies is switched on

★

A man holds a bicycle wheel and walks into a cathedral

In the middle of summer, a band-aid has melted on the asphalt

A wooden swan sits in a bakery, its back hollowed out and filled with loaves
of bread

A wasp picks up a single grain of rice, disappears, then returns to pick up an-
other grain

The dark clouds are darker through the skylight of a limousine

★

When its master blows down a cardboard tube, the dog cocks its head to one
side

A wire coat-hanger is found lying in the snow, and later on, a slice of white
bread

A man sells oranges in front of an empty field that stretches towards the ho-
rizon

On the beach at night, as the fire dies down, the sound of the ocean increases

★

A jogger runs past with *Stop Acid Rain* printed on his tee-shirt

In the crowded men's room, all three toilet doors change from 'occupied' to
'vacant' at the same time

At a serious accident, an ambulance arrives before the tow trucks

The letters on a tomato sign are the same red as the tomatoes

When the corn field is harvested, the hedgerows rustle with mice

★

At the airport, baggage tickets hang from the circular light above the check-in desk

A steel girder casts its shadow across the side of a concrete building

A gust of wind sends the cellophane from a cigarette packet high up into the evening sky

On a late-night bus, an old man smelling of beer manages to complete a crossword puzzle

A cat slips between two candles without singeing its tail

★

Cleaning under his bed, a writer finds his lost pen covered in dust

In the archaeological museum, a series of crystalline *pings* are heard when the lights are switched on

Two painters in white overalls each stand on a white ladder and paint the same building white

In the Japanese garden, a carp with a human face glides by

On a corrugated iron roof, a seagull opens and closes its beak

★

A pile of cigarette butts lies at the end of a long pier

In a house by the sea, a man in his night-shirt is changing a light-bulb

In the hair salon, a small girl places two red plastic straws in her hair

An empty cassette box shines like a pool of water on a dark bedspread

The shadow of a cat sits on the shadow of a fence

★

Outside a tropical hotel, a hotel worker is struck by a large leaf

A young mother drives around the block until her babies are fast asleep

A chandelier of icicles hangs from the underside of a rusted fire-escape

Light shines through a blowfly as it settles on a television screen

Lotuses are opening under high-tension wires

★

An ice-cream van breaks down right beside a waterfall

A dog barks, and snow falls from a tree

[2005]

Richard von Sturmer was born in Devonport, on Auckland's North Shore, and was educated at Westlake Boys' High School and Auckland University.

In the late 1970s he wrote songs for several New Zealand music groups: The Plague, Blam Blam Blam and Avant Garage. His first play, *The Green Lion*, was performed at 100m² in Auckland in 1980, after which he wrote performance pieces and toured New Zealand and Australia with Charlotte Wrightson as The Humanimals. In 1986 his second play, *The Search For Otto*, was staged in the Auckland School of Architecture's design theatre.

His first book, *We Xerox Your Zebras*, a collection of prose-poems, appeared in 1988, followed by *A Network of Dissolving Threads* in 1991. In 1992 he left New Zealand to undertake ten years of Zen training at the Rochester Zen Center, a Buddhist Community in upstate New York. There he collaborated with photographer Joseph Sorrentino on a third book, *Images From The Center*, writing seven essays on Zen practice. He also edited *Zen Bow*, the Rochester Zen Center's quarterly publication, 1993–2002.

In 2003 he returned to live and work in Auckland and in mid-2003 received the *brief* Writer's Award for a two-month writer-in-residency on Great Barrier Island.

POETRY:

We Xerox Your Zebras. Auckland: Modern House, 1988.
A Network of Dissolving Threads. Auckland: Auckland University Press, 1991.
Images From The Center. New York: Rochester Zen Center, 1998.
Suchness: Zen Poetry and Prose. Wellington: HeadworX, 2005.

ROMA POTIKI (B. 1958)

[CD 2.44] **Exploding Light**

Let that one exploding light
move out over us,
define the landscape.

In spring
there's peat bog heaped up,
new mountains appear on Paekakariki beach –
Tane Mahuta distributing packages
Old God, come in again from Whanganui.

Children tumble through the wooded sea
draw the cold ocean through their nostrils,
spit into the soup where life spills
over the jugular horizon.

14 year old boy/men splay themselves at the reaches
cough and shout at the sea –
get lippy to a bigger sound
enjoy the early splash of a returning tide,
good dogs in a gentle season.

Girls laugh and screech,
hidden in their togs
stretched outward and waiting.
Gulls circle.

Back at the house
they tell stories –
'And he was trying to kiss her. And her
little sister whacked him with her towel
and he ran away, ha ha ha.'

And he ran all the way
to heaven,
his own pulse driving him
harder than the manic cadence
of all the girls, burning.

I keep hearing rain in the gutters.

Reach down,
inside every love
is the slap of fluid and salt tongues,
new songs in drifts –
dresses, piu piu and swaying fibres.

Eartha Kitt says *'You're sweet my dear . . . Like a girl that's never been kissed.'*

That's right –

the band plays on at fever pitch
full of light and angled rhythms and gorgeous
chaos flung at our feet.

Rimbaud never booked a single ticket,
he just kept the door open –
water floods in,
patterns keep heaping up,
laid over each other
every body
that ever bled in summer
bark stripped back
to show love's new skin
glowing,

we recognise
ourselves,
every broken piece,

the children we once were.

[2002]

For Paiki

The news came to me that you had left us.
The phone messages said you were dead.

I do not understand you are dead.

A star-lit manu aute hangs above you; soon you will be the one
skimming the land, looking at the last reach of our mother's body
where spikes of red flame blaze into two oceans, swirling.

In the deep bush your nakedness shines.
In that place a hundred shades of green
float around you, feathers fall through the air,
tupuna spill chants into your open ears, the caress of recognition.

You are making bird tracks in the sky, you are walking quiet above us,
you are practising your taiaha at night so's not to wake us.
You are very old, like the river that is a language,
you are the silence that precedes first light.

You haven't changed at all, always could move easy,
slip between the rise and fall of a shadow
to surprise us with your presence.

I will not find you at your grave,

I will find you resting near a favourite tree
or sitting quietly on the wharf at twilight
or whispering to me from the hot sand.

Now you are not here
you appear at a crowded party,
you are seen at the roadside beside the train tracks
or I find you suddenly as I walk the hills.

With these words
I search for what I know but cannot.
Sleep leaves me as I wait for the stroke of your voice.

We are remembering you
with every story,
with every movement of earth as we gather,
with every tear

crying for you

for our own aloneness.

Taken from us 8.12.98

[2002]

Riven   [CD 2.46]

I am dead, dead
gone, gone –

as insubstantial as a cloth of mist up from the river
I drift towards rafts of bones
needles, eyes-of-needles.

The chills of night overtake me
and I hear no sound
except the small interruption, for a second,
of the river's clack as I slip from the bank
numbed. All about me water,
I am riven, dispersed.

An émigré,
I pass
becoming a continuous lilting note
swaying, swaying,
as I enter the sparking mountain.

My tongue splits
and I have the loudest of voices
beyond this everydayness.

Fire-rocks crack my back and hips,
in my open mouth, cinders
from the volcano.

Hot trees fall
and smiling
I receive each flame.

Past the tears of fathers, of mothers,
freed
to stare into the light
all about me,

I am riven, dispersed.

[2002]

Roma Potiki was born in Lower Hutt in 1958, of Te Rarawa, Te Aupouri and Ngati
Rangitihi descent, and was educated at Wainuiomata College. Her first collection of
poetry, *Stones in Her Mouth*, appeared in 1992. She has since had three other volumes
published: *Roma Potiki* (1995), *Shaking the Tree* (1998) and *Oriori* (1999). In 2000, she was
one of twelve poets to have new work commissioned for the 'Parihaka: The Art of
Passive Resistance' exhibition at the City Gallery, Wellington. Potiki is also a prominent
playwright and has contributed significantly to the development of Maori theatre.

POETRY:
Stones in Her Mouth. Tamakimakaurau: IWA, 1992.
Roma Potiki. Wellington: Wai-te-ata Press, 1995.
Shaking the Tree. Wellington: Steele Roberts, 1998.
Oriori: A Maori Child is Born: From Conception to Birth. Paintings by Robyn Kahukiwa.
    Auckland: Tandem, 1999.

PLAYS:
[with He Ara Hou]. *Ta Matou Mangai*. Ed. Hone Kouka. Wellington: Victoria University
    Press, 1999.

PROSE:
Memory Walking, Wellington: City Gallery, 1998.

TRACK LIST

ABBREVIATIONS

(1974) Waiata Archive, CDs 1–27: reel-to-reel tapes of original Waiata recording sessions, copied onto CDs (stored in the Alexander Turnbull Library, Wellington and Auckland University Library's Special Collections)

(2004) Aotearoa New Zealand Poetry Sound Archive, CDs 1–40 (recordings stored in Auckland University Library's Special Collections and the Alexander Turnbull Library)

GW   Going West Books & Writers Festival Recordings Archive

nzepc   New Zealand Electronic Poetry Centre Archive, www.nzepc.auckland.ac.nz/

SV   *Seeing Voices* (Auckland: Auckland University Press, 1999)

*   Variations between recorded poem and published copytext

TRACK / TITLE		TIME	SOURCE OF RECORDING
CD ONE			
Peter Olds (b. 1944)			
1.1*	Waking up in Phillip Street	2.21	27.5 (2004)
1.2*	Doctors Rock	1.18	14.13 (1974)
1.3	Elephant	2.01	27.4 (2004)
Bernadette Hall (b. 1945)			
1.4	Party tricks	0.54	15.37 (2004)
1.5	The Lay Sister	1.04	15.40 (2004)
1.6	Famine	0.55	15.42 (2004)
1.7	Amica	0.48	15.36 (2004)
Stephanie de Montalk (b. 1945)			
1.8	Tree Marriage	1.19	9.29 (2004)
1.9	Northern Spring	1.14	9.34 (2004)
Alan Brunton (1946–2002)			
1.10*	The Man on Crazies Hill	3.34	10.8 (1974)
1.11*	*from* Waves	4.57	nzepc (1994)
Sam Hunt (b. 1946)			
1.12*	My Father Scything	0.48	5.35 (1974)
1.13*	Rainbows and a Promise of Snow	1.39	17.25 (2004)
1.14*	Hey, Minstrel	1.11	17.30 (2004)
1.15*	*from* Plateau songs	1.09	17.33 (2004)
1.16*	Bottle to Battle to Death	2.16	17.35 (2004)
Bill Manhire (b. 1946)			
1.17	The Old Man's Example	0.16	4.17 (1974)
1.18	Domestic	0.42	23.17 (2004)
1.19	On Originality	1.24	23.18 (2004)
1.20	Visiting Mr Shackleton	0.38	23.19 (2004)
1.21	Miscarriage	0.42	23.20 (2004)
1.22	Valedictory	1.02	23.21 (2004)
1.23	A Song about the Moon	1.23	23.22 (2004)
James Norcliffe (b. 1946)			
1.24	at Franz Josef	0.53	26.24 (2004)
1.25	planchette	0.42	26.26 (2004)
1.26	the visit of the dalai lama	0.38	26.19 (2004)

Ian Wedde (b. 1946)

1.27	Earthly: Sonnets for Carlos 31	0.52	14.34 (1974)
1.28	Earthly: Sonnets for Carlos 32	1.00	14.35 (1974)
1.29	Earthly: Sonnets for Carlos 35	0.56	14.38 (1974)
1.30*	Barbary Coast	4.57	38.8 (2004)

Fiona Farrell (b. 1947)

1.31	Anne Brown's Song	1.09	12.30 (2004)
1.32	Instructions for the Consumption	3.29	12.39 (2004)

Keri Hulme (b. 1947)

1.33*	*from* Fisher in an Autumn Tide	5.18	GW (1997)

Murray Edmond (b. 1949)

1.34*	Voyager	7.41	11.34 (2004)

Jan Kemp (b. 1949)

1.35	Against the softness of woman	1.09	13.5 (1974)
1.36*	Jousting	1.33	21.13 (2004)
1.37	The sky's enormous jug	1.03	21.5 (2004)
1.38	Sailing boats	0.27	21.7 (2004)
1.39	'Love is a babe'	0.59	21.16 (2004)

Cilla McQueen (b. 1949)

1.40*	Living Here	2.21	24.22 (2004)
1.41	Fuse	2.30	24.25 (2004)

CD TWO

Bob Orr (b. 1949)

2.1*	The X	0.37	22.15 (1974)
2.2*	A Country Shaped Like a Butterfly's Wing	2.05	28.11 (2004)
2.3	Ballad of the Great South Rd	0.50	28.17 (2004)
2.4*	Eternity	1.41	28.20 (2004)

Geoff Cochrane (b. 1951)

2.5	Spindrift Sunday	0.46	07.52 (2004)
2.6	1988	1.01	07.56 (2004)
2.7	Zigzags	2.16	07.57 (2004)
2.8	Atlantis	0.48	07.59 (2004)

Bill Sewell (1951–2003)

2.9	Jahrhundertwende	0.58	33.5 (2004)
2.10	Riversdale	0.53	33.9 (2004)
2.11	Breaking the quiet	1.35	33.10 (2004)
2.12*	Censorship	1.43	33.15 (2004)

David Eggleton (b. 1952)

2.13*	Poem for the Unknown Tourist	2.35	12.4 (2004)
2.14*	Teen Angel	1.23	12.5 (2004)

Graham Lindsay (b. 1952)

2.15	Playground	0.56	22.30 (2004)
2.16*	Cloud silence	1.18	22.34 (2004)
2.17	Life in the Queen's English	0.51	22.36 (2004)
2.18	Chink	2.49	22.41 (2004)

Iain Sharp (b. 1953)

2.19*	Amnesty Day	2.55	33.21 (2004)
2.20	Two Minute Poem	2.08	33.27 (2004)

Janet Charman (b. 1954)

2.21	'they say that in paradise'	0.31	07.35 (2004)
2.22	ready steady	0.47	07.36 (2004)
2.23*	from wake up to yourself	0.17	07.39 (2004)
2.24	but she wanted one	0.46	07.44 (2004)
2.25	cuckoo in the nest	1.01	07.46 (2004)
2.26	injection	0.51	07.48 (2004)

Paula Green (b. 1955)

2.27	greek salad	0.15	15.1 (2004)
2.28	oven baked salmon	0.12	15.2 (2004)
2.29	afternoon tea with Virginia Woolf	0.30	15.3 (2004)
2.30*	Two Minutes Westward	2.27	15.9 (2004)

Vivienne Plumb (b. 1955)

2.31	A Letter from my Daughter	2.14	29.1 (2004)
2.32	The Vegan Bar and Gaming Lounge	1.22	29.2 (2004)
2.33	The Tank	1.04	29.3 (2004)

Apirana Taylor (b. 1955)

2.34	Sad Joke on a Marae	1.13	36.48 (2004)
2.35	Parihaka	2.09	36.50 (2004)
2.36	Hinemoa's daughter	1.47	36.54 (2004)
2.37	six million	1.02	36.58 (2004)

Anne French (b. 1956)

2.38	The new museology	1.35	SV.13 (1999)
2.39*	Trout	1.27	GW (2005)
2.40*	Acute	1.15	GW (2005)
2.41	Uncle Ron's last surprise	1.10	GW (2005)

Michele Leggott (b. 1956)

2.42	cairo vessel	8.09	nzepc (2006)

Richard von Sturmer (b. 1957)

2.43*	Dreams	5.11	37.40 (2004)

Roma Potiki (b. 1958)

2.44	Exploding Light	2.26	29.12 (2004)
2.45*	For Paiki	2.11	29.14 (2004)
2.46	Riven	1.22	29.16 (2004)

VARIANT READINGS

PETER OLDS
Waking up in Phillip Street [1.1]:
l. 9: a drum-kit in the house over the back fence
ll. 11–12: or Buddhism! (What's wrong with getting off
your face occasionally, anyway?)
l. 18: Anorectic ghosts at night on the stairs (lit by street lamps)
l. 23: looking for Sandy, Jack, the kitten – a cigarette.
l. 26: in the communal kitchen; or the cat-strangling lies
['*Oh, Baxter is Everywhere*' (Square One Press, 2003) 20–21]

Doctors Rock [1.2]:
l. 23: through the broken flattened hedges
l. 32: your silent King Grandad grin.
[*It was a Tuesday Morning* (Hazard Press, 2004) 41–42]

ALAN BRUNTON
The Man on Crazies Hill [1.10]:
l. 89: i'll send no letters
[*The Young New Zealand Poets* (Heinemann Educational Books, 1973) 29–31]

from Waves [1.11]:
ll. 1–147: so you want to know
Memm
therefore
lend undestructed ears,
I'll do this haha just once more . . .

in a shingle shack lit by candles
way out back among the muters,
the town was Brightwater,
a kaka went in flight between the window
and the golden moon,
the Earthly Guest was born,
his mother 'beautiful as a wreck of paradise'
dreamed him in her skirt of dust,
dreamed him beneath the open sky,
dreamed her little anomaly on a mallow eating fire,
dreamed him as geometry, as I over I, what always
is:
dreamed the Unremembered Dream
where One
in a black cloud
comes upon the unrepresented world
beginning as a 'grainy glow',
morning star and vesper star
and downward tear of light.
Papa came running, the hurrying man,

hurrying from the swingle at the mill
where he swinked for swinish gods
in the city of tents
on Wailing Creek
where it meets Burning Creek
and Glossopteris grows;
the poebird above him
chortled in the beeches as he ran:
Hurry hurry!
He called his boy Ernest
(Rutherford)
but Ernie neither heaven learned nor chaos
from his father's lips

     first words, God
     who knows eh Memm

The boy picked up magnets
lying on the Urth and melaphyres,
and
one March when turnstones filled the sky
at night in his sack
he picked up transmissions from Siberia;
he was the odd bod at school –
sometimes, in the middle of a match,
he sank to his knees
and drew universals in the sandy pitch
(like Archimedes, QED:
'once a quantity moves it will not rest').
E.R. was good,
he was Head Boy, valedictorian and dux
and, set for bigger things,
lithely made his way to Canterbury
while the dew yet clung to the grass.
In that godly city
they gave him the gownroom
to work at *solve & coagula*
with copper wires and sealing lacs
for he was
'Diligent in the use of his hands . . .'
and that was as far as he could go at that time,
whispereth he in Papanui
'Mary, Mary . . .'
in his pyjamas
sneaking down the corridor

     it stands to reason
     Memm
     you don't need the Band of Hope
     to tell you

if you know the question,
that the world's all a continuity
along parameters set centuries ago,
you need no glazed
optic tube
Memm, to tell you that

his part of the planet was flat
but not wide enough for an Abode
so
E.R. goes to work in the fields
with air in his purse
at the edge of the Empire expanding
out, breaking up the clods
like in Hesiod,
hoeing at the haulms with a scuffle
in the black frost before sunrise
but, as the sun influences the sky
and digs into the dirt,
his brother came hippity-hop
in his iron boot
(his crippled shadow stuttering behind):
'Ernie, there's this letter.'
Standing up, the big man tore the seal,
    Greetings
    Rutherford
    The Crystal Palace wishes to assist you
    in the attainment of your
    ultimate beehood
    therefore please exhibit yourself
    before the Queen
    &c., &c., &c.
In that ploughed field on that day
prime matter opened up its gates,
E.R. chucked his spade and damned
'That's the last spud I will ever dig!'
and subsequent to farewells
to his Ma on the tennis-court
he beggared down the quickened road
with all his fingers popping,
he was bound for Bassorah

    you could say, Memm
    Uranos
    was looking out
    for his boy

From the burning deck
to England O
he looked back on stooks of ambrite

where Nestor's sails were furled
To England
without the littlest of regrets
To Englan
to do service to the Queen
with his 'radi   os'
To Engla
on a ship with hoggets stacked below
To Engl
cursing P & O
To Eng
to live for six weeks on Humid Way
completely non fingo
To En
during a heat-wave in sunny South Kensington,
he slipped on a banana skin ha ha
rickety knees for the rest of his life!
To E
came a gram from J.J.:
'Come to the Cam and live with us.'
He always went the shortest distance,
he walked to Cambridge in a week,
took a room in Trinity,
campestral in the Fen.
He could almost smell neutrinos
dropping from magellanic clouds
like that as they got up his nose.

[*Moonshine* (Bumper Books, 1998) 41–45]

SAM HUNT

My Father Scything [1.12]:

l. 8:   working the path through the lupins toward the sea.

[*Collected Poems 1963–1980* (Penguin, 1980) 45]

Rainbows and a Promise of Snow [1.13]:

ll. 6–8:   Or so life's been for me this last
           half-life of sixteen years. Days go
           so very slow they say, so fast.

l. 15:   Sixteen and just left school

l. 23:   I got to the river, friend,

l. 28:   so very fast, so slow:

[*Collected Poems 1963–1980* (Penguin, 1980) 193–94]

Hey, Minstrel [1.14]:

l. 13:   It wasn't till after we buried you

l. 17:   gave up the piss.

l. 36:   touch the moon, that's okay too.

[*Down the Backbone* (Hodder Moa Beckett, 1995) 30–31]

Plateau songs [1.15]:

l. 3:   took a room further down
l. 23:   And your best poem? he asked.
l. 30:   or ski or tramp or do
                    [Colin Hogg, *Angel Gear* (Heinemann Reed, 1989) 4]

Bottle to Battle to Death [1.16]:

ll. 1–2:   From Bottle to Battle to Death,
             the places where we lived from
l. 30:   We stalked each other, minute by minute.
ll. 37–40:   And to say I loved you was true.
             And that I hated you was true.
             I thought though, if we lie down,
             lie down low, we may come through.
l. 49:   Or, maybe best we call it a day.
                    [*Running Scared* (Whitcoulls, 1982) 26]

IAN WEDDE
Barbary Coast [1.30]:

l. 92:   Almost gaily. The ship sailed on.
                    [*The Drummer* (AUP, 1993) 17–19]

KERI HULME
from **Fisher in an Autumn Tide** [1.33]:

l. 10:   an unwary glance   see! sunlight
ll. 12–13:   see! torch flick
             blinds, I see nothing except that obscuring flare
l. 38:   any kind of light; sneering at – but I tied that straggly black
                    spider myself, mate,
ll. 45–46:   (call it fishtorture as an animal-rights cousin of mine does if you're so inclined;
             that neither upsets me nor enlightens me, having figured out early . . .
ll. 48–49:   stumbling round life)
             but you're basically playing or
l. 70:   Hours drift by before I realise they've evanesced.
l. 81:   clamp arteries, just hooks, tiny hooks, this hook I've defanged and now
l. 85:   until drawn to the dubious safety of a net. She weighs
l. 87:   and she danced so well.
l. 96:   That hen, lost in the brown distance, felt wet cotton gloves but never suffered
l. 98:   suffering, who can tell? I can't hear fish scream or moan either.
                    [*Stonefish* (Huia, 2004) 53–58]

MURRAY EDMOND
Voyager [1.34]:

l. 19:   the 4000 islands of the city of Stockholm
l. 20   and all of these regrets and all of these repentances
l. 77   the body washed up on the shore
l. 103:   in the David Montham Air Force Base near Tucson Arizona
l. 110:   and one there stood with an ironic lean
l. 121:   scrolled down through paragraphs of text
l. 124:   so that it could have been
                    [*Fool Moon* (AUP, 2004) 53–58]

JAN KEMP
Jousting [1.36]:
l. 11:   haranguing her between Mission Bay fountain
ll. 21–22: who never did nor ever tried –
            how she still favours him.

[*Dante's Heaven* (Puriri Press, 2006) 83]

CILLA MCQUEEN
Living Here [1.40]:
l. 1:   Well you have to remember this place

[*Crīk'ey: New and Selected Poems* (McIndoe, 1994) 24–25]

BOB ORR
The X [2.1]:
ll. 1–2:   Looking across
            the rd where the tobacconist
l. 8:   on the mattress / the drunk
ll. 10–14: is again trying to borrow $1.00
            off me to buy some wine /
            Steve shoots
            marmite / Neil pretends
            he's Christ

[*Big Smoke* (AUP, 2000) 190]

A Country Shaped like a Butterfly's Wing [2.2]:
l. 23:   watch clouds like a caravan of camels sauntering across the horizon

[*Valparaiso* (AUP, 2002) 15]

Eternity [2.4]:
l. 9:   like scales that tilt toward injustice –
l. 11:   like some surreal craft now cut adrift by phantom boatmen.

[*Valparaiso* (AUP, 2002) 45]

BILL SEWELL
Censorship [2.12]:
l. 1:   where the truth would make a difference

[*The Ballad of Fifty-One* (HeadworX, 2003) 49–50]

DAVID EGGLETON
Poem for the Unknown Tourist [2.13]:
l. 18:   built for the end of the golden wether;
l. 26:   corkscrewing rides and water cannon,

[*Rhyming Planet* (Steele Roberts, 2001) 10–11]

Teen Angel [2.14]:
ll. 9 & 18–19:   [*no refrain*]

[*Rhyming Planet* (Steele Roberts, 2001) 18]

GRAHAM LINDSAY
Cloud silence [2.16]:
l. 12:   it seemed like home
                              [*The Subject* (AUP, 1994) 24–25]

IAIN SHARP
Amnesty Day [2.19]:
l. 30:   Prices triple come 9.30. I arrive at 9.25.
l. 40:   it's Amnesty Day! I'm meant to read at Riemke's shindig.
                         [*The Singing Harp* (ESAW, 2004) 22–23]

JANET CHARMAN
from **wake up to yourself** [2.23]:
part-title: v. the drive to work
ll. 7–8:   [left out]
                        [*Cold Snack* (AUP, 2007) 11–14]

PAULA GREEN
Two Minutes Westward [2.30]:
ll. 43–44: *ritorniamo nel chiaro mondo?*
                        [*Crosswind* (AUP, 2004) 4–5]

ANNE FRENCH
Trout [2.39]:
l. 15:   crew handling, weather, the Gulf, sailing
                      [*Wild* (AUP, 2004) 10–11]

Acute [2.40]:
l. 2:   It is cool and remote, an instrument. Beneath
                      [*Wild* (AUP, 2004) 58]

RICHARD VON STURMER
Dreams [2.43]:
l. 44:   Lotuses are opening beneath high-tension wires
                      [*Suchness* (HeadworX, 2005) 110–13]

ROMA POTIKI
For Paiki [2.45]
ll. 20–21   or in the sea at night
              or whispering near me in the hot sand.
                      [author variant, 2007]

BIBLIOGRAPHY

PRIMARY TEXTS:

Big Smoke: New Zealand Poems 1960–1975. Ed. Alan Brunton, Murray Edmond and Michele Leggott. Auckland: Auckland University Press, 2000.

Brunton, Alan. *Moonshine*. Wellington: Bumper Books, 1998.

Charman, Janet. *Snowing Down South*. Auckland: Auckland University Press, 2002.

Charman, Janet. *Cold Snack*. Auckland: Auckland University Press, 2007.

Cochrane, Geoff. *Into India*. Wellington: Victoria University Press, 1999.

Cochrane, Geoff. *Acetylene*. Wellington: Victoria University Press, 2001.

de Montalk, Stephanie. *The Scientific Evidence of Dr Wang*. Wellington: Victoria University Press, 2002.

Edmond, Murray. *Fool Moon*. Auckland: Auckland University Press, 2004.

Eggleton, David. *Rhyming Planet*. Wellington: Steele Roberts, 2001.

Farrell, Fiona. *Cutting Out*. Auckland: Auckland University Press, 1987.

Farrell, Fiona. *The Inhabited Initial*. Auckland: Auckland University Press, 1999.

French, Anne. *Boys' Night Out*. Auckland: Auckland University Press, 1998.

French, Anne. *Wild*. Auckland: Auckland University Press, 2004.

Green, Paula. *Cookhouse*. Auckland: Auckland University Press, 1997.

Green, Paula. *Crosswind*. Auckland: Auckland University Press, 2004.

Hall, Bernadette. *Heartwood*. Christchurch: Caxton Press, 1989.

Hall, Bernadette. *The Persistent Levitator*. Wellington: Victoria University Press, 1994.

Hall, Bernadette. *Settler Dreaming*. Wellington: Victoria University Press, 2001.

Hall, Bernadette. *The Merino Princess: Selected Poems*. Wellington: Victoria University Press, 2004.

Hogg, Colin and Sam Hunt. *Angel Gear*. Harmondsworth: Heinemann Reed, 1989.

Hulme, Keri. *Stonefish*. Wellington: Huia, 2004.

Hunt, Sam. *From Bottle Creek*. Wellington: Alister Taylor Ltd., 1972.

Hunt, Sam. *Collected Poems 1963–80*. Auckland: Penguin, 1980.

Hunt, Sam. *Running Scared*. Christchurch: Whitcoulls, 1982.

Hunt, Sam. *Down the Backbone*. Auckland: Hodder Moa Beckett, 1995.

Kemp, Jan. *Against the Softness of Woman*. Dunedin: Caveman Press, 1976.

Kemp, Jan. *The Sky's Enormous Jug: Love Poems Old & New*. Auckland: Puriri Press, 2001.

Kemp, Jan. *Dante's Heaven*. Auckland: Puriri Press, 2006.

Leggott, Michele. *Milk & Honey*. Auckland: Auckland University Press, 2005.

Lindsay, Graham. *Big Boy*. Auckland: Auckland University Press, 1986.

Lindsay, Graham. *The Subject*. Auckland: Auckland University Press, 1994.

Lindsay, Graham. *Lazy Wind Poems*. Auckland: Auckland University Press, 2003.

Manhire, Bill. *Collected Poems*. Wellington: Victoria University Press, 2001.

McQueen, Cilla. *Crık'ey: New and Selected Poems 1978–1994*. Dunedin: John McIndoe, 1994.

McQueen, Cilla. *Soundings*. Dunedin: University of Otago Press, 2002.

Norcliffe, James. *Rat Tickling*. Christchurch: Sudden Valley Press, 2003.

Norcliffe, James. *Along Blueskin Road*. Christchurch: Canterbury University Press, 2005.

Olds, Peter. *'Oh, Baxter is everywhere': Some Dunedin Poems*. Dunedin: Square One Press, 2003.

Olds, Peter. *It was a Tuesday Morning: Selected Poems 1972–2001*. Christchurch: Hazard Press, 2004.

Orr, Bob. *Blue Footpaths*. London: Amphedesma Press, 1971.

Orr, Bob. *Valparaiso*. Auckland: Auckland University Press, 2002.

Parihaka: The Art of Passive Resistance. Ed. Te Miringa Hohaia, Gregory O'Brien and Lara
　　Strongman. Wellington: Victoria University Press, 2001.
Plumb, Vivienne. *Avalanche*. Wellington: Pemmican Press, 2000.
Plumb, Vivienne. *Nefarious*. Wellington: HeadworX, 2004.
Seeing Voices. Auckland: Auckland University Press, 1999.
Sewell, Bill. *Making the Far Land Glow*. Dunedin: McIndoe, 1986.
Sewell, Bill. *El Sur*. Wellington: Pemmican Press, 2001.
Sewell, Bill. *Erebus: A Poem*. Christchurch: Hazard Press, 1999.
Sewell, Bill. *The Ballad of Fifty-One*. Wellington: HeadworX, 2003.
Sharp, Iain. *The Singing Harp*. Paekakariki: Earl of Seacliff Art Workshop, 2004.
Taylor, Apirana. *Eyes of the Ruru*. Wellington: Voice Press, 1981.
Taylor, Apirana. *Soft Leaf Falls of the Moon*. Auckland: Pohutukawa Press, 1996.
von Sturmer, Richard. *Suchness: Zen Poetry and Prose*. Wellington: HeadworX, 2005.
Wedde, Ian. *Earthly: Sonnets for Carlos*. Akaroa: Amphedesma Press, 1975.
Wedde, Ian. *Driving Into the Storm: Selected Poems*. Auckland: Oxford University Press, 1987.
Wedde, Ian. *The Drummer*. Auckland: Auckland University Press, 1993.
The Young New Zealand Poets. Ed. Arthur Baysting. Auckland: Heinemann Educational Books,
　　1973.

SECONDARY TEXTS:
Complete with Instructions. Ed. David Howard. Christchurch: Firebrand, 2001.
The Globe Tapes. Ed. Michael Morrissey, Mike Johnson and Rosemary Menzies. Auckland:
　　Hard Echo Press, 1985.
The New Poets: Initiatives in New Zealand Poetry. Ed. Murray Edmond and Mary Paul.
　　Wellington: Allen & Unwin New Zealand and Port Nicholson Press, 1987.
New Zealand Electronic Poetry Centre. Available at: http://www.nzepc.auckland.ac.nz/
New Zealand Literature File. The University of Auckland Library Website. Available at:
　　http://www.library.auckland.ac.nz/subjects/nzp/nzlit2/authors.htm
New Zealand Writers. The New Zealand Book Council Website. Available at:
　　http://www.bookcouncil.org.nz/writers/index.html
The Oxford Companion to New Zealand Literature. Ed. Roger Robinson and Nelson Wattie.
　　Melbourne: Oxford University Press, 1998.
The Oxford History of New Zealand Literature in English. Ed. Terry Sturm. 1991. 2nd edition.
　　Auckland: Oxford University Press, 1998.
The Penguin Book of Contemporary New Zealand Poetry: Ngā Kupu Tītohu o Aotearoa. Ed. Ian
　　Wedde, Miriama Evans and Harvey McQueen. 1985. Auckland: Penguin, 1989.
The Penguin Book of New Zealand Verse. Ed. Ian Wedde and Harvey McQueen. 1985. Auckland:
　　Penguin, 1987.
Private Gardens: An Anthology of New Zealand Women Poets. Ed. Riemke Ensing. Dunedin:
　　Caveman Press, 1977.
Real Fire: New Zealand Poetry of the 1960s and 70s. Ed. Bernard Gadd. Dunedin: Square One
　　Press, 2001.